THE FACTS ABOUT TMJ

DID YOU KNOW:

- TMJ pain afflicts ten million Americans—eight million of them women.

- You may see a dentist, an oral surgeon, a physical therapist, an orthopedist, and a psychiatrist—all to treat the same TMJ dysfunction.

- In most patients, pain can be completely eliminated without surgery or medication.

- Certain professions or habits can cause or aggravate TMJ disorders.

The information in this book is your best weapon against TMJ. You'll discover that for most patients, the treatments are simple and inexpensive. You'll find everything you need to know in . . .

**RELIEF FROM
CHRONIC TMJ PAIN**

THE DELL MEDICAL LIBRARY:

RELIEF FROM CHRONIC BACKACHE
RELIEF FROM CHRONIC HEADACHE
RELIEF FROM CHRONIC TMJ PAIN
RELIEF FROM CHRONIC ARTHRITIS PAIN
LEARNING TO LIVE WITH CHRONIC IBS
LEARNING TO LIVE WITH CHRONIC FATIGUE SYNDROME

THE DELL MEDICAL LIBRARY

Relief from
Chronic
TMJ Pain

Antonia van der Meer

Foreword by Steven B. Syrop, D.D.S.

A LYNN SONBERG BOOK

Published by
Dell Publishing
a division of
Bantam Doubleday Dell Publishing Group, Inc.
666 Fifth Avenue
New York, New York 10103

ISBN: 0-440-20628-6

Printed in the United States of America
Published simultaneously in Canada

June 1990

10 9 8 7 6 5 4 3 2 1

OPM

ACKNOWLEDGMENTS

Thanks to the following for their time, expertise, information, and advice:

American Dental Association, Chicago, Illinois.

Dr. Neil Gottehrer, D.D.S., director of the Craniofacial Pain Center, Abington, Pennsylvania, and faculty member, New York University, College of Dentistry/TMJ and Craniofacial Pain Center.

Dr. Steven Roser, D.M.D., M.D., associate professor and director of Oral and Maxillofacial Surgery at Columbia Presbyterian Medical Center and member of the Executive Committee of Temporomandibular Joint–Facial Pain Clinic at Columbia Presbyterian Medical Center, New York City.

Dr. Steven Syrop, D.D.S., director of the Temporomandibular Joint–Facial Pain Clinic at Columbia Presbyterian Medical Center, New York City; assistant professor of dentistry at Columbia University School of Dental and Oral Surgery. Dr. Syrop also maintains a private practice in New York City.

Meralee Guhl, P.T., registered physical therapist, staff physical therapist with the TMJ–Facial Pain Clinic at Columbia Presbyterian Medical Center, and private practitioner in New York City.

CONTENTS

FOREWORD by Steven Syrop, D.D.S.   1

INTRODUCTION   4

ONE   WHAT IS TEMPOROMANDIBULAR JOINT
      DISORDER?   6

      The Temporomandibular Joint
      The Nature of TMJ Pain

TWO   DO YOU HAVE A TMJ DISORDER?   13

      TMJ Disorder Symptoms
      The Ambiguity of TMJ Disorder Symptoms
      A Self-Assessment Quiz

THREE   WHAT CAUSES TMJ DISORDERS?   19

      A Bad Bite
      Stress
      Bad Posture
      Arthritis
      Trauma to the Joint
      Poor Dental Work
      The Gender Issue

FOUR   WHERE TO GET HELP   28

      Where to Begin
      The TMJ "Specialist"
      TMJ Clinics

Pain Treatment Centers
TMJ Support Groups
Treatment Costs

FIVE   DIAGNOSIS   37

Visiting a Doctor or Dentist
The Medical History
The Physical Examination
Other Tests
Conservative Treatment as a Diagnostic Tool
Painful Pretenders
A Precise Diagnosis

SIX   TREATMENT   51

Physical Therapy
Orthodontics
Trigger Point Injections
Nutrition
Soft-Food Diet
Medication and Drug Addiction
Permanent Improvements

SEVEN   SURGERY—THE FINAL FRONTIER   76

Qualifications for Surgery
Before Surgery
Types of Surgery
Questions to Ask Before You Undergo Surgery
Finding the Right Surgeon
A Word About Insurance

EIGHT   COPING WITH PAIN   87

Chronic Pain Patients
The Effect on the Family

Stress Reducers
Rebuilding Your Life
Future Dental Care

NINE A FEW CASE HISTORIES   94

Love at First Bite
Getting to the Tooth of the Matter
A Disc in Time
The Long and Winding Road
Aspirin Free
Grinding to a Halt
A Surgical Answer

CONCLUSION   101

GLOSSARY   102

FOREWORD

In my private practice and as director of a large TMJ–facial pain clinic, I continually deal with people suffering from chronic pain, from the moderate to the unbearable.

Often, they have suffered and been searching for answers for months or even years. Some have seen several physicians or dentists without relief of their symptoms.

They come asking:

• What is causing the pain?

• Is there something seriously wrong?

• How can I get relief?

• Will I ever feel pain free again?

• How drastic is the treatment?

• How long will the treatment take?

These people suffer from temporomandibular joint disorders although TMJ disorders are common, most people are only just beginning to learn about them and to understand their causes and treatment.

Facial pain is a complicated matter. It has numerous causes, and frequently more than one factor is responsible. Facial pain symptoms mimic the symptoms of many medical disorders.

While teaching about and treating this complex problem, I concluded that one principle stands out as the single most important aspect of any treatment. That is that the patient must understand the diagnosis and rationale for the treatment. The patient needs to learn what is causing the discomfort, how it started, what aggravates it, and what makes it better. Anxiety about one's medical condition only magnifies the original problem. Understanding the cause of the pain helps relieve it.

This book allows TMJ sufferers to learn about their problem in an understandable fashion. This knowledge is crucial to getting better. Only a well-informed patient can make appropriate treatment choices.

The good news for TMJ sufferers is that most patients improve with simple treatment. Desperate flights to irreversible treatments such as tooth capping are both unnecessary and unwise, in most cases. Most patients require only conservative, noninvasive, reversible treatment that centers on exercise, simple appliances, and pain management. Arthroscopy and surgery, where appropriately indicated, can also be very successful.

This book will answer the questions, allay the fears, educate sufferers and their families, and assure them that there is hope.

STEVEN B. SYROP, D.D.S.
Director, Temporomandibular
Joint–Facial Pain Clinic
Columbia Presbyterian Medical Center
New York City

INTRODUCTION

Millions of Americans, either knowingly or unknowingly, suffer from TMJ disorders. This book addresses those sufferers and offers them hope for relief—relief from their often relentless pain; relief from their headaches, neckaches, and other associated symptoms; relief from their nightmare of not knowing what is wrong; relief from their suspicions that the pain is "all in their head."

If you suffer from a TMJ disorder, this book will help you better understand the problems you face. It offers ways to overcome the pain that plagues you. It explains the physiology of the temporomandibular joint—how it works, what can go wrong with it, and why. It leads you through the various tests and exams that aid in the diagnosis of TMJ disorders. Most important, it tells you *how you can help yourself.* It lists the treatments that are currently available and the best places to go for dental and medical assistance. You will find out about physical therapy, bite correction, massage, relaxation therapy, medications, bite plates, and new surgeries that may be an option for you. And you will learn how to keep the problem from recurring.

Although not all sufferers will find complete relief from their ailment, most *can* be helped. The pain you experience now can be reduced or eliminated. It's time to end the confusion, leave behind the myriad treatments that have not yet been of any help, and find out how *you* can overcome the debilitating effects of temporomandibular joint disorders, as others have.

With the help of this book, you can get on with your life and relieve your pain, and you may even permanently correct your condition.

A.V.D.M

WHAT IS TEMPOROMANDIBULAR JOINT DISORDER?

Temporomandibular joint (TMJ) disorder is a disorder of the jaw joint that usually causes unexplained and persistent pain. It is a broad, blanket term that refers to a wide variety of facial pain problems and a constellation of symptoms all related in some way to the dysfunction of the temporomandibular joint.

TMJ disorders are much more common than one might think. About ten million Americans suffer from them. This means that about one person in twenty knows the pain and discomfort of a TMJ disorder. The American Dental Association believes that the figure is actually much higher and that TMJ disorders may affect as many as sixty million Americans. If you are a TMJ sufferer, you may be heartened to know that you are far from alone.

TMJ disorders affect four times as many women as men. No one knows why this is so. Women between the ages of fifteen and forty-four are the most likely to experience a TMJ disorder.

TMJ disorder is frequently misunderstood and often misdiagnosed. It has been nicknamed "the great impostor" and "the painful pretender" because of its uncanny ability to mimic other conditions and diseases. One reason that TMJ disorders are hard to diagnose is that jaw-joint disorders can send pain radiating out to other parts of the body.

Usually, there has been a previous injury or injuries to the jaw joint or muscles, and this sets the stage for the resulting TMJ disorder. Specific TMJ problems range from retrodiscitis (a painful inflammation in the tissue of the joint) to muscle spasm to a slipped disc in the jaw joint to arthritis. Your dentist will be able to give you a more specific diagnosis that pinpoints the exact problem, but you will learn all about these various disorders as you read this book.

THE TEMPOROMANDIBULAR JOINT

The jaw joint, medically known as the temporomandibular joint, is one of the most flexible joints in the whole body. It is made up of bones, muscles, soft tissues, and nerves. The jaw joint's main purposes are to allow efficient chewing and movements for speech. Its amazing flexibility allows humans to make the wide range of sounds necessary for oral communication.

The simple act of chewing is actually rather complicated. The jaw must move not only up and down but forward and back and from side to side. The neck and back muscles are connected directly or indirectly with the chewing muscles of the temporomandibular joint.

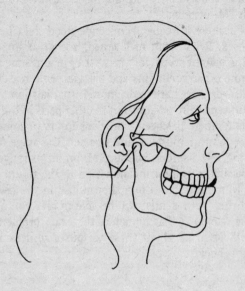

The TM joint is the hinge that connects the two main parts of the human skull, the cranium and the mandible. The *cranium* is the part of the skull that contains the brain. The part of the cranium that lies just in front of the ears is the *temporal bone*. The *mandible* is the U-shaped bottom jaw bone. We are able to make varied chewing movements with our jaws because of two rounded knobs, known as condyles that are located just in front of the ears at the ends of the mandible. These knobs rotate within depressions in the temporal bone called the *articular fossa*. To feel the TM joint, place your fingers on the sides of your head, at the front of each ear. Now open and close your mouth. When you clench your teeth, you'll be able to feel it as high up as your temples, as well as in your cheeks.

In order to understand TMJ disorder, you should know a few more details about this complex part of your anatomy. A special disc called the *articular disc* sits on top of each condyle. Attached to the disc are the sensitive *retrodiscal tissues*. The discs and tissues act as shock absorbers and prevent friction between the temporal bones and condyles. If the articular discs slip out of place, this causes the clicking and popping noises associated with many TMJ disorders.

Ligaments are the connective tissues that help control the movement of the jaw so that the condyles don't slip and so that the jaw doesn't open too wide. Some of the ligaments form a capsule that surrounds the joint. This capsule produces fluid that lubricates the joint to ensure that it works smoothly and efficiently. Inside the capsule are many blood vessels and nerves that can be very sensitive to pain.

The chewing muscles, or *muscles of mastication*, stretch from the cranium to the mandible on each side of the head. They are attached to the jaw bones by *tendons*, or connective tissues. Two sets of chewing muscles are used: one set opens the jaw and another closes it. The muscles that are responsible for closing the jaw are stronger than the ones that open it. When you chew, your chewing muscles move your jaws up, down, forward, back, and side to side. Other muscles, in the neck and back, are also connected with chewing.

Nerves control sensations in the joint. Some nerves work to control the muscles; others feel pressure and pain. The feeling neurons are called *sensory nerves*. They pick up and send pain messages to the brain if there is any damage to the nerves or surrounding tissue. Fatigue and inflammation will also stimulate a neuron to send a pain message to the brain. The nerve that runs through the TMJ joint is called the *auriculotemporal nerve*. Like all nerves, it is made up of neurons that control the muscles and tissues and those that feel.

The job of the *teeth* is, of course, to chew food. The upper teeth are connected to the skull; the lower teeth are in the lower jaw, or mandible. The top and bottom chewing surfaces of the teeth should all make contact with one another. The cutting teeth of the upper jaw should slightly protrude over the bottom cutting teeth.

When properly aligned, the chewing system works well. Unfortunately, teeth come in all shapes and sizes and may not fit well inside certain mouths. They may be crooked; some teeth may be broken or missing. These irregularities can cause a *malocclusion*, or bad bite. Malocclusion can become a major cause of TMJ disorders. In fact, anything that interferes with the correct working of the TM joint can cause a TMJ disorder.

THE NATURE OF TMJ PAIN

Pain is the most common and obvious symptom of a TMJ disorder. About 85 percent of TMJ sufferers feel pain on only one side of the head. As many as 25 percent experience pain in their shoulders. Nearly half feel pain either constantly or at least once a day.

The pain of TMJ is very hard to live with because it is a head pain. Head pain is virtually impossible to forget or ignore. It occupies you and worries you. Furthermore, because the TM joint is so crucial to everyday life, it is hard not to use it. Unlike pain somewhere else in your body—such as in the knee, which you could respond to simply by not bending it or by putting the leg up for a rest—pain in the temporomandibular joint cannot be given a rest.

Our individual pain thresholds determine the way we perceive the pain of a TMJ disorder. Usually, you feel pain where your problem lies. The neurons in the temporomandibular joint, for example, send pain messages to the brain when there is damage, fatigue, inflammation, muscle spasm or any other problem in that area.

But pain may also be felt in an area far from the actual site of an injury. Unfortunately, the brain does not always correctly identify where the pain is located. For example, heart attack patients may experience pain in the arm or shoulder instead of in the heart. A pain that actually originates in the TMJ joint may be perceived by you as a pain in your neck, tooth, ear, or head. A problem with your neck or shoulder muscles may be felt in your face, or pain originating in your face may be perceived by you to be in your ear. No one really understands this phenomenon; the pathway of pain in the body is simply not always direct.

To further complicate the issue, a change in the way one muscle in your body works can affect other muscles in your body. Thus, a spasm in the chewing muscles may in turn refer pain to areas outside the jaw, causing a spasm in the neck or back muscles. This referral of pain may lead both patient and doctor to search for problems in the back or neck instead of in the TM joint.

Because the nature of TMJ pain is elusive, many patients suffer with no relief. They often travel from doctor to doctor and from treatment to treatment. They may begin to think that their problems are "all in their heads." A doctor who looks for a source of back, neck, or head pain and finds nothing may even agree. Your pain can appear to be unfounded.

Since TMJ has recently become well publicized and much talked about, fewer practitioners now overlook it as a diagnostic possibility. Happily, this translates into better care for you—and a prompter end to your pain.

Once you know about TMJ disorders, you will be able to take charge of your life again and overcome feelings of despair. There is a reason for your pain! There are solutions to the syndrome that will leave you pain free!

TWO

DO YOU HAVE A TMJ DISORDER?

TMJ sufferers experience a wide variety of symptoms. In this chapter, you will discover what some of these most typical symptoms are. Many of them may be familiar to you and relate to your pain. Equip yourself with this information, and seek a diagnosis from a reputable dentist. This chapter will steer you in the right direction. It is not meant for self-diagnosis.

TMJ DISORDER SYMPTOMS

TMJ pain can be elusive and maddeningly difficult to diagnose. When should you suspect that a TMJ disorder may be the source of your pain? Tip-offs include:

- a noticeable clicking sound when you open and close your jaw

- a clicking sound combined with pain

- pain or tenderness when you open and close your jaw or when you chew

- pain in the jaw that worsens when you yawn

- limited jaw movement

- pain in the temple or cheek

- facial pain

- earache, "stuffy" ears, or ringing in the ears

- headache pain that doctors are unable to diagnose

- dizziness

- stiff or aching shoulders

- pain in the neck muscles

- unexplained backache (very rare)

- toothache with no apparent cause (beware, though— about 99 percent of people who complain of tooth pain have tooth problems, not TMJ disorders)

These symptoms may also change. They may get worse, get better, overlap, or recur.

If you suffer from one or more of these symptoms, TMJ disorder is a diagnostic *possibility* that you and your doctor may want to explore. None of the above symptoms mean you definitely have a TMJ disorder. Almost all of them could just as easily be signs of problems unrelated to the TM joint.

Furthermore, one symptom alone—such as clicking of the jaw—with no other associated problems or pain is not enough for a diagnosis of TMJ disorder. The symptoms of TMJ disorder are so common that almost everyone experiences one of them at some time or another. And, of course, not everyone has TMJ disorder! A dentist can help you to determine whether your symptoms are actually TMJ related. If necessary, your dentist will refer you to a dentist who is also a TMJ specialist. (See chapter 4 for more on where to find help.)

THE AMBIGUITY OF
TMJ DISORDER SYMPTOMS

Let's look in more detail at some of the most common symptoms of TMJ disorder and what they might mean.

Headaches

Many things can cause a headache. One of the most common types is the tension headache. The tension headache is a result of muscle contractions in the head and neck muscles. Tension headaches are described as generalized aches, as opposed to pounding or throbbing pain. They may result from a recent episode of tension or fatigue or from jaw clenching, which stresses the muscles of the face, neck, and head. They are not related to disease.

Clicking or Popping

A normal, healthy jaw joint makes no noise when it moves. If you hear clicking or popping when you open your jaw or chew food, you may be hearing the sound of your disc slipping in and out of its proper position. This may or may not prove that you have a problem or need treatment, however.

Grinding Noise

If you hear a grating sound like sandpaper when you open and close your mouth, it may be the sound of your bones rubbing together. It's possible that the disc and its fluid cushion are not in the right position, or that the fluid has dried up and little or no cushion is left, or even that the disc has ruptured. Without proper cushioning, the rough bones rub together and produce the grinding sound.

Sore Jaw Muscles

Normal use of the jaw should not cause any muscle soreness. If you are experiencing sore jaw muscles, this may be a sign that the muscles are being strained by improper use or overuse.

Pain Around the Ear or Face

This pain is often a referred pain that stems from a problem in the temporomandibular joint. The same is often true of pain felt in the head, neck, or shoulder.

Locking of the Jaw

If your jaw sticks or locks in place when you open it, this may be a sign of an internal derangement. The disc may have been displaced, thereby preventing the jaw from fully opening or closing.

A SELF-ASSESSMENT QUIZ

Answer these questions with yes or no:

1. Do you suffer from chronic headaches?

2. Do you have pain in the neck, shoulders, face, or teeth?

3. Is your pain worse upon waking?

4. Is your pain worse when you talk a lot?

5. Do you feel more pain when you eat? (Is it especially uncomfortable when you eat chewy foods such as bagels?)

6. Do you experience a feeling of sinus congestion or pain behind your eyes?

7. Are you unable to fully open and close your mouth?

8. Do you hear clicking from your TM joint?

9. Place your fingers on your temples and press gently. Do you feel any pain?

10. Place your fingers on your forehead. then on the base of skull and behind the jawbone. In each place, press gently but firmly. Do you feel pain?

11. Open your mouth as wide as you comfortably can. Are you unable to insert more than two fingers in the space between your teeth?

12. Do you have trouble moving your jaw freely from side to side and from front to back?

13. Stand in front of a mirror and watch your mouth as it opens and closes. Does it pull to one side or another?

If you answered yes to many of these questions, you should make sure that your dentist or physician considers TMJ disorder as a possible diagnosis.

THREE

WHAT CAUSES TMJ DISORDERS?

The TM joint is complex and highly intricate. When perfectly balanced, it works beautifully. But there are many potential problems in a system that is so delicately balanced. Many things can go wrong. If any single part of the multifaceted chewing system breaks down, a TMJ disorder can result. Perhaps this is one reason why so many millions of people experience TMJ-related problems.

No one knows exactly what causes TMJ disorders, but we can point to a number of contributing factors, from stress to trauma, from poor posture to disease.

A BAD BITE

Everyone has irregularities and imperfections in their mouths. The body usually compensates for these, with no resulting problems. Sometimes, however, a bad bite or malocclusion can cause a painful TMJ disorder. (Actually, scientific studies have not yet proven a direct, causal relationship between malocclusion and TMJ, but some dentists have noted a connection based on clinical experience.)

The causes of a bad bite include:

- missing teeth

- worn teeth

- congenital problems

- dental treatment (caps or crowns that are too high or low)

- orthodontic treatment

Malocclusion strains the muscles of the jaw joint. Some of the muscles end up working harder than others. Muscles in the jaw can become stiff, sore, and tired, the same way that overworked muscles in other parts of the body can. Occasionally, the overworked muscle will go into a spasm, causing more pain. Muscles in the head, neck, and back work to try to compensate for and alleviate this pain. This strains them in turn and can cause the neck, head, and back pain that is so often associated with TMJ problems. This is referred to as *myofascial pain dysfunction*, or MPD.

Malocclusion, if severe, can also directly affect the position of the condyles. This in turn causes pressure on the bone of the articular fossa. The surrounding soft tissues can also be irritated and injured.

STRESS

Stress and tension in our daily lives are often unavoidable. Feelings of worry are universal. The way each person responds to these stresses, however, is unique. Some people can cope with no apparent difficulties. Others get headaches or ulcers as a result of their nervous reaction to stressful situations. In some people, stress factors can eventually trigger health problems.

One reaction to stress can be clenching or grinding the teeth. Why do people clench or grind their teeth when they are under stress? Part of the reason may involve the way the human nervous system was built to handle stress many millennia ago. Threats to people's well-being caused and still cause a physical response—adrenaline kicks in, we breathe more quickly, and muscle tension increases. The body is set either to fight or to flee. We no longer fight life's stresses in a physical way—our enemy may now be a mortgage payment instead of a mastodon. But our bodies continue to react the way the bodies of early humans did.

As the muscles contract and tense during times of stress, some people react by constricting their facial muscles and clenching their teeth. Not everyone responds this way and no one knows why some people do and some do not. There is no personality sketch that can be drawn of the typical TMJ sufferer. Physicians have noted, however, that many clenchers and grinders appear to be anxious, with a tendency toward perfectionism. They may seem calm and controlled, but they often have strong feelings bottled up inside that they are unable to admit to or express.

People may come to clench and grind their teeth habitually, whether some of the time or all the time. Many people do not even realize that they are clenching or grinding their teeth. They may do so while they sleep.

In the normal resting position for the mouth, the lips are closed and the jaws are slightly parted. There should be no pressure on the teeth at this time. When teeth are clenched, they do not rest. The only time pressure should be applied to the teeth is when a person bites, chews, or swallows.

Constant clenching and/or grinding eventually tire the muscles of the jaw. Excessive grinding and clenching can even cause the articular disc to become displaced. If this happens, the popping and clicking noises associated with TMJ disorder will be heard. Persistent, worsening clicking may indicate that the disc is being squeezed farther forward. The disc may actually roll off from its normal place on top of the condyle and get in front of it.

This can cause the jaw to lock and prevent you from opening your mouth past a certain point. Normal chewing and speech can become impossible. Often (but not always), this is coupled with pain. At first, the jaw may "lock" only occasionally, but locking will recur with greater frequency if not treated. Friction on the disc and its attached tissues can actually cause the tissues and disc to break apart. The temporal bone, no longer protected from the condyle by the disc, becomes worn and damaged. The bone can begin to deteriorate.

Muscle fatigue that results from clenching causes its own problems and pain. It most commonly results in myofascial pain dysfunction. Muscle spasms can occur, and pain can spread to nearby muscles.

Sometimes the grinding is severe enough to change in

the shape of the teeth and the bite. When this occurs, the grinding results in a malocclusion, which in turn causes muscle fatigue and possible TMJ disorders.

Of course, not everyone who clenches or grinds their teeth develops a TMJ problem. As many as 90 percent of people may occasionally grind or clench their teeth. The question is, are there any other painful symptoms associated with it?

If stress-related clenching and grinding are at the root of your problems, you can find ways to kick the habit. (See chapter 6 for relaxation tips and stress-reducing ideas.)

BAD POSTURE

By itself, bad posture is unlikely to cause TMJ disorder, but in conjunction with another TMJ-related factor, it can aggravate TMJ disorder and tip the balance toward pain and problems. If you hold your head too far forward or too far back, its weight can put undue strain on your neck and back muscles—and these tired muscles can become stiff and sore and cause pain. A nearsighted person may thrust his or her head forward to read; a secretary might develop a forward thrust from trying to see a video display terminal more clearly. This position strains the muscles of the neck, back, and TM joint. The soft tissues of the joint can then become inflamed. People who often cock their heads to one side or who speak on the phone by holding the receiver between their ear and shoulder are also inviting muscle trouble.

A physical therapist can train you to avoid these postural problems and lessen your chances of aggravating TMJ disorder symptoms.

ARTHRITIS

Osteoarthritis, which results from wear and tear on the joint, is not an uncommon cause of TM pain. Although flare-ups may normalize on their own, when they don't treatment is needed. Less commonly, rheumatoid arthritis can effect the TMJ joint, as it does other joints in the body. (Lupus, an autoimmune disease, is even more rarely at the root of TMJ problems.) Even though arthritis of the temporomandibular joint is rare, an X-ray may be taken to determine whether you suffer from rheumatoid arthritis. Usually, rheumatoid arthritis would be found in your other joints as well.

TRAUMA TO THE JOINT

An injury to the temporomandibular joint can cause a TMJ disorder. Accidental injury can occur during a fall or in a fist fight. The most common form of accident, of course, is an automobile accident, which can injure the TM joint by a direct blow to the jaw or by whiplash (a fast, snapping action of the neck).

A hard blow to the jaw can shove the bottom jawbone backward with force. The condyles may be forced back into the retrodiscal tissue attached to the disc. This can cause *retrodiscitis*, a painful inflammation of the sensitive retrodiscal tissues. There may be side effects as well, such as myofascial pain and referred pain. You may experience chronic headaches for weeks or even months. If the injury to the retrodiscal tissues causes bleeding, more serious problems may result, including stiffness of the jaw joint. A permanent stiffening or restriction of the joint may result if you do not receive treatment early on. In some rare cases, the joint can even become frozen (known as *ankylosis*). In these cases, the only treatment may be surgery.

The sudden, violent neck movements of whiplash can cause damage to the temporomandibular joint as surely as a direct hit can. There may be no direct impact to the jaw, but trauma results nevertheless. As the head whips back, the jaw opens too widely and the joint is strained. When it whips forward, the jaw slams shut violently. Sometimes, the jaw can actually become dislocated or the disc displaced. The appearance of the symptoms may be delayed, making it difficult for the patient to associate the accident with the later TMJ problems.

Trauma may also result from wide mouth movements. For example, yawning too widely and even shouting with a wide-open mouth have been known to trigger TMJ disorders. This, however, is quite rare. Unfortunately, opening the mouth too widely in the dentist's chair is not uncommon. Root-canal work or surgery may require that the mouth remain open for prolonged periods, and sometimes the practitioner may force it open too widely. Under anesthesia, a patient may be unaware of just how far the mouth is open, as the discomfort that accompanies this cannot be felt. The muscles are relaxed and offer no resistance to the opening. Such trauma can result in inflammation or, in severe cases, disc displacement.

A mouth that is too tightly closed is also traumatic to the joint. For example, someone in traction for a back injury may receive too much pressure on the jaw during therapy. Today, physicians take greater care with traction slings because they are more aware of TMJ disorders. The slings used today do not put so much pressure on the temporomandibular joint.

POOR DENTAL WORK

Poor dental work can also cause some of the problems related to TMJ disorder. A high spot on a filling, for example, may create a bad bite, which in turn may create jaw problems. A cap or crown that is too high can also unbalance the bite and lead to a TMJ disorder. Orthodontic treatment (such as braces to straighten teeth) may be another source of trouble if it creates an uneven or uncomfortable bite. Dental treatment that does not take the TM joint into account may cause a TMJ disorder by putting a strain on the joint and its muscles.

THE GENDER ISSUE

Being female obviously doesn't *cause* TMJ disorders, but it is interesting that as many as 75 to 80 percent of TMJ patients are women. A number of theories have tried to explain this phenomenon. One theory is that women are simply more comfortable with the idea of seeking treatment when they have pain than men are. According to this theory, women find it more socially acceptable to admit having pain or a health problem. They may also be more willing to make the time to seek treatment. Men may feel they have no time for such "coddling." Some men may think that they should "tough it out" and live through the pain rather than admit it is too much to bear.

A second theory suggests that women may have looser ligaments, and that this may be the reason why they have TMJ disorders more frequently than men. As of yet, there is no scientific proof of this. It is interesting, however, that the incidence of TMJ disorder in women who have mitral valve prolapse (a heart murmur caused by the loosening of the ligaments that hold the mitral valve of the heart) is high. This, however, is only a nonscientific observation. No one really knows why women suffer from TMJ disorders in greater numbers than men.

If you think you may be suffering from a TMJ disorder, you'll want to turn to a practitioner for a proper diagnosis and immediate help.

FOUR

WHERE TO GET HELP

For a TMJ-related problem, the best medical specialist you can see is a dentist. Unfortunately, because TMJ disorders mimic other illnesses, patients often search for help in the offices of other medical specialists.

At first, you may not have suspected you had a TMJ problem and so turned to any number of specialists in several different fields. Depending on your symptoms and their sensitivity, you may have seen a chiropractor, a masseuse, a psychiatrist, or an ear, nose, and throat specialist. During the various treatments, counseling, and tests you received, you may have experienced some short periods of relief from pain—only to have it return again. This is because you have not yet been to the one specialist who *can* help you—a dentist who is also a TMJ expert.

Traveling from specialist to specialist with no cure in sight can be extremely frustrating and depressing. As a reader of this book, you obviously suspect that you are suffering from a TMJ-related problem. This chapter explains how to find a dentist who can give you the help you need to get your life back on track again.

WHERE TO BEGIN

In general, start with your general practitioner when you have a health concern. But if you suspect you have a TMJ disorder, you'll also want to see someone who deals with TMJ patients daily.

If your main symptoms involve headache pain, a visit to a neurologist should perhaps come first. There are many headache types that should be considered before you jump to the conclusion that you have a TMJ disorder.

If earache is your main symptom, see an ear, nose, and throat specialist first. He or she can determine whether you suffer from an infection or other medical problem related to the ear, nose or throat.

Is your neck or upper back giving you the most trouble? A visit to an orthopedist or chiropractor could be warranted.

Once you have ruled out a few other possible diagnoses, make an appointment with a dentist who deals regularly with TMJ disorders.

THE TMJ "SPECIALIST"

There is currently no recognized TMJ-disorder specialty. It is not taught as a separate specialty in dental schools; there are no boards (exams to certify doctors and dentists in specialized fields) that can be taken in the TMJ field.

Dentists receive their training informally, from other practitioners. At the moment, there is little or no regulation of who may refer to themselves as a TMJ specialist. TMJ specialists are essentially self-named.

For this reason, among others, it can be very difficult to determine which practitioner you should choose. Here are some suggestions for finding the right help:

• Contact your local chapter of the American Dental Association for a referral.

• Call a nearby dental school.

• Contact a teaching hospital and ask if they can recommend an expert in the treatment of TMJ disorders.

• Look for a TMJ center connected with a dental school or hospital. A center provides the benefit of a team of specialists.

• Consider the severity of your symptoms. You may not need either a team of doctors or a self-proclaimed TMJ specialist. The treatment of most TMJ disorders is within the realm of your regular dentist. He may be able to diagnose and treat your problem himself.

• If your regular dentist is uncomfortable handling TMJ disorders, ask him for a recommendation. He may know of a dentist who would be better able to help you.

Questions to Ask a Dentist

When you make an appointment with a dentist, try to get some general information before you proceed very far. You might want to ask the following questions:

- Where did you learn about TMJ disorders?

- What percentage of your practice is TMJ related?

- What types of diagnostic tests do you usually suggest?

- What types of treatment plans do you offer?

- Do you work with any support people, such as physical therapists, or headache specialists?

- What do you charge?

- How long will treatment take?

- What percentage of your patients find pain relief?

Unscrupulous Practitioners

Unfortunately, some dentists and doctors in the world are entrepreneurs. When they see a TMJ disorder, they see dollar signs. These people may know little about your problem but are happy to take your money. Some tip-offs that might make you suspicious about a particular caregiver include:

- *Excessive testing.* If you feel that your doctor has been giving you numerous fancy and expensive tests without good reason, you may begin to question that doctor's sincerity. (See chapter 5 for help in determining whether too many tests are being done.)

- *Minimal testing.* Nor should a doctor make a diagnosis on the basis of one test alone. For example, a dentist who does only an electromyography test and on the basis of that concludes you have a TMJ disorder is not being thorough. Usually, a diagnostic test is useful if it adds information, but a diagnosis based on only one test is not very valuable.

- *Poor listening.* If the doctor doesn't bother to get a complete health history from you or doesn't take the time to listen to your symptoms, complaints, and thoughts, he is probably not going to give you an accurate diagnosis. The doctor who skips this important portion of the examination and jumps straight to a diagnosis of TMJ disorder might not be trustworthy.

- *No explanations.* A reputable doctor explains his diagnosis and treatment plan, as well as his prices, to his patients.

- *Radical treatment.* If a dentist wants to *begin* with radical treatment (treatment that alters your bite, irreversibly changes your mouth or jaw structure, or involves surgery), you should seek other opinions.

- No relief. If you have no relief from your pain after six months of therapy, you should seriously consider changing practitioners. Speak to the dentist about the problem, and if you don't get a satisfactory answer, seek help elsewhere. You shouldn't stay with someone who gives no help.

Once you have chosen a dentist, make sure that you always understand the diagnosis and treatment. The treatment should make sense to you. If you do not understand it, you should not have it done. The practitioner should be able to tell you honestly about how much time the treatment will take and what it will cost you before he begins treatment.

TMJ CLINICS

You may wish to contact a TMJ clinic for help. These clinics are often affiliated with a teaching hospital or medical school. One major benefit of a TMJ clinic is that there you are treated by a team of experts, as opposed to a single dentist. The team may consist of some or all of the following:

- a general dentist

- an oral and maxillofacial surgeon

- an orthodontist

- a psychiatrist or psychologist

- a physical therapist

- a biofeedback specialist

- a neurologist

- a headache specialist

If the clinic is associated with a hospital or a dental school, they usually are able to call on a number of other specialists and experts, including ear, nose, and throat doctors, radiologists, eye doctors and others. These specialists can be called in to give an opinion on your case. Because of the diagnostic difficulties sometimes involved with TMJ disorders, this can be especially helpful and time-saving for the patient.

PAIN TREATMENT CENTERS

TMJ patients who suffer from chronic pain may want to consider going to a pain treatment center. These centers house complete management teams skilled in the art of controlling pain.

Specialists from a number of different fields may treat you. Like TMJ clinics, pain treatment centers are often affiliated with hospitals or medical centers. To find a pain treatment center, ask your dentist for a referral, or contact a university hospital or medical center for the name of a reputable clinic near you. The cost of treatment varies from center to center.

Although these centers can help you deal with pain, you may still need a dentist skilled in the treatment of TMJ disorders to establish a diagnosis and work in conjunction with the pain center. Even after you are pain free, the underlying problem with your joint may remain, but many people feel that there is no reason to make any other changes or undergo any further treatment.

TMJ SUPPORT GROUPS

TMJ sufferers have banded together in various regions to create informal support groups. They meet and discuss common problems, such as the effect of the TMJ pain on their lives, their search for treatment, the return to a normal, pain-free life. Some people find a support group very helpful because it removes them from the isolation of their medical problem. Suddenly, they are surrounded by people who feel the pain they themselves feel, know the frustration they know, and live the life they lead. Talking to someone in a similar situation can make it much easier to bear.

Ask your practitioner if he or she knows of a support group in your area. If there is none, you might want to let your dentist or therapist know that you are interested in starting one (if you have the energy!). Your practitioner could spread the news among other patients or allow you to post a sign announcing your group's first meeting.

TREATMENT COSTS

Treatment costs vary from patient to patient and from case to case. Much depends on how long your treatment takes and what procedures are being used to stop the pain and/or correct the underlying problem. The bottom line, however, is that TMJ treatment can be expensive.

Not all insurance policies cover TMJ treatment, so this cost may be yours to bear alone. One source of coverage confusion is that a TMJ disorder is multidisciplinary. It is a dental problem; yet it is also an orthopedic problem because it is a joint. At the same time, it is a medical condition, with symptoms reaching outside the dental area. Therefore, the treatment you receive is also multidisciplinary. For this one problem, you may see a dentist, an oral and maxillofacial surgeon, a physical therapist, and a psychiatrist!

Insurance coverage for TMJ treatment is therefore unpredictable. Check with your insurance carrier for specific information regarding your claims. Explore all the options. If your dental coverage does not include TMJ treatment, be sure to check your medical coverage. A splint, for example, is an orthopedic appliance and as such may be covered under your medical policy. Surgical treatments often are covered, even if nonsurgical treatments are not.

As TMJ disorder becomes more widely accepted and talked about, insurance companies should begin to make better coverage available. In the meantime, patients often end up bearing the brunt of the costs. For many, though, it is more than worth the price to live pain free.

FIVE

DIAGNOSIS

TMJ disorder has only recently been defined, but suddenly it seems that "everyone" has it. Why the sudden popularity? Is it being overdiagnosed? While it is possible that TMJ disorder is being overdiagnosed these days, the increase in TMJ cases is due mainly to increased awareness of its existence as a problem.

A lot of health problems have symptoms similar to those of TMJ disorder, so no one—patient or doctor—should immediately leap to the conclusion that TMJ disorder is the correct diagnosis. But with better diagnostic tests, a greater ability to treat the problem successfully, and greater public awareness of the syndrome, we are sure to see and hear about more and more cases of TMJ disorder.

VISITING A DOCTOR
OR DENTIST

At first, your condition and complaints may appear to your dentist to be a giant jigsaw puzzle with thousands of pieces. A dentist should be able to see broad outlines of the picture after talking with you for a half hour or an hour. To a physician, the puzzle may seem more complicated than it does to a dentist. But as the medical community becomes increasingly aware of TMJ disorder, medical physicians will be increasingly likely to suspect it and refer patients to dentists. (See chapter 4 for information on finding help for TMJ disorder.)

The dentist will take your medical history—listening to you and reviewing and screening your medical forms. He or she will give you a complete physical examination before making any evaluation or decision about your jaw.

THE MEDICAL HISTORY

Your dentist should begin by taking your complete medical history. He or she will probably ask many questions about the pain you are experiencing and about the problems you are complaining of. At the TMJ–Facial Pain Clinic at Columbia-Presbyterian, an entire team of specialists examines this medical history. The staff believes that if they listen to a patient long enough, *the patient* will make the diagnosis. You play an important role in the doctor/patient relationship. Good communication and honesty on your part, combined with good listening on the part of the dentists and doctors, are crucial to an accurate diagnosis of your problem.

At your first visit, you will probably be asked, among other things:

- When did the illness begin?

- Did the onset of your pain occur at the same time as an accident?

- Have you been involved in an accident that may have caused trauma to your back, neck, or jaw? Have you ever been in a car accident? When?

- Describe the pain you experience.

- What is the duration of the pain?

- Is the pain chronic or intermittent?

- What time interval is there in between painful periods?

- What makes the pain better? (certain foods, weather)

- What makes the pain worse? (eating, yawning, stress)

- Does your pain occur in a pattern? (during stressful times? in relation to your menstrual cycle?)

- Does light bother you?

- Does the jaw hurt more when you move it or use it?

- What other specialists have you consulted about this problem? What diagnoses or treatments were you given by these specialists?

- What medications have you taken in your search for pain relief?

- Do you grind or clench your teeth?

- Have you ever had braces?

- Have you ever had surgery? If so, for what and when? Was it performed under general anesthesia?

- Have you had oral surgery or root-canal work?

- Have your wisdom teeth been removed? Have any other teeth been pulled? Why?

- Do you wear glasses? For what problem? Have you ever had your eyesight tested?

- Has your hearing ever been tested?

- Do you suffer from allergies?

As you can see, you will be asked many questions that are not about the jaw at all. You may be asked about sensitivity to light, for example, because this is a telltale sign of migraine. You may be asked if your pain is menstrually related—TMJ problems are not. These questions help to determine if your problem is a non-TMJ condition, such as an ear problem, eyestrain, migraine, or premenstrual syndrome (PMS).

THE PHYSICAL EXAMINATION

Next, the dentist will do a physical examination, testing the range of your jaw motion and pinpointing the areas of pain, of stiffness, or of limitation of movement. The dentist *palpates* (presses on) the joint to see if there is any pain or tenderness. If you are suffering from muscle spasm, the dentist's applied pressure probably won't cause you any pain. If your joint is inflamed, however, there is a good chance that you will feel pain right over the joint when he presses. The dentist would then palpate the muscles of the jaw to see if *they* hurt. If you feel no pain when the dentist presses the joint or the muscle, the dentist may suspect that your problem lies somewhere outside the jaw area.

To test the full range of jaw movement, the dentist will ask you to open your mouth, stretching as wide as you can without pain. Both *active* and *passive ranges of movement* (AROM and PROM) are tested. AROM is your ability to open your own mouth by yourself. PROM is the range of movement the dentist can achieve while moving your jaw with his hands.

As you open and close your mouth, the dentist may use a stethoscope or a Doppler to listen for clicking, which can indicate that the articular disc is slipping out of place. If there is clicking, the dentist can measure the severity of the problem by determining when the opening click occurs. If the opening click is early, the problem is less serious than if the opening click is late. Likewise, a late closing click is less serious than an early closing click. (Clicking does not necessarily mean that treatment is warranted. Sometimes it goes away by itself.)

The dentist might also examine your ears, oral cavity, throat, cranial nerves, sinuses, eyes, and nose. If an ear problem is suspected (for example, if you are complaining of hearing loss or pressure in your ears), the dentist will refer you to an ear, nose, and throat doctor for an exam. Buzzing or ringing in the ears and clogged ears may both be related to TMJ, but they can just as easily be unrelated to TMJ disorder. If you have clogged ears and a physician finds that your hearing is normal, the dentist will return to a TMJ-related theory and search further for the right diagnosis. Ear exams are often an important part of TMJ testing and diagnosis.

You will also be checked for tooth problems, such as cavities. A problem that appears to be TMJ related may actually be a simple tooth problem. Just by looking at the surfaces of your teeth, the dentist can usually tell if you have been grinding them. There are telltale signs of the wear and tear grinding causes. Patients are often wholly unaware that they have this habit (they may grind in their sleep), so it is important for the dentist to check you for grinding even if you do not think you do this.

Most of the time, whether you have one symptom or many symptoms, a diagnosis can be made by listening to the patient and performing an examination.

OTHER TESTS

Occasionally, additional data are needed to determine a difficult diagnosis, to gauge the severity of the problem, to see how treatment is working, or to rule out non-TMJ-related diagnostic possibilities. Unfortunately, some dentists routinely suggest a battery of tests (perhaps because they are afraid of being sued and want documentation). Whenever a test is suggested to you, make sure you understand why it is being suggested and what information it will give the dentist.

The following tests might be suggested to TMJ patients under different circumstances:

X Rays

X rays are often ordered early on in the search for diagnostic clues. They may be taken to get a clear look at the bone structure of the jaw and detect gross abnormalities. An X ray may be suggested if there is limited movement of the jaw, noise in the joint, or a history of arthritis. Jaw X rays would be taken from several different vantage points: with teeth clenched, with the jaw relaxed, and with the mouth open. X rays of the teeth show cavities, which may be at the root of your pain. X rays do expose you to some radiation. A lead shield should be used to protect any body parts not being X-rayed. Since everyone is concerned about overexposure to radiation these days, X rays are never used without reason. Pregnant women should avoid X rays, as the exposure can be dangerous to the fetus.

Stethoscope Exam

Most dentists use a simple stethoscope to get information about the joint. This exam is accurate but not costly. More rarely, a dentist may use a digital or computerized stethoscope. In some cases, the dentist might use a Doppler, an instrument that magnifies sounds. This noninvasive technique can pick up and magnify your jaw-joint sounds.

CAT Scan

A CAT scan is a highly sophisticated form of X ray. (As such, it involves radiation, although less than a normal X ray.) A computer receives the information from the X-ray beams and reconstructs an image of the area. Black, gray, and white areas show bones, fluids, organs, and tissues. The image is viewed on a television monitor, but it can also be printed out. A CAT scan lasts only about a half hour from start to finish.

The CAT scan is considered one of the least effective tests for diagnosing TMJ disorders because it is difficult to see the articular disc with it. Because of the sophistication of the machinery, its effectiveness also depends on the radiologist using the equipment. Some radiologists are very knowledgeable about the TM joint and can get an excellent picture on the disc. You will have to depend on your dentist's estimation of the resources, machines, tests, and practitioner skills in your area.

Magnetic Resonances Imaging (MRI)

MRI provides a good picture of the soft tissues of your jaw joint, including the articular disc. MRI is considered to be diagnostically superior to the CAT scan in TMJ cases since the CAT scan cannot give detailed information about the soft tissues the way the MRI can. It involves no radiation and is thought to be safe.

Not all MR images are of high quality; some machines are more powerful and take better pictures. The right software, the right equipment, and the right radiologist can make an enormous difference in the quality of the test. Your dentist should be able to recommend the best MRI located in your area.

MRI is expensive and not readily available in all areas of the country, so it is usually suggested only if no diagnosis can be made from the history and exam. It would also be used to confirm a diagnosis for which surgery is the suggested treatment. An MRI test is used on probably less than five percent of patients.

Some patients find the MRI process uncomfortable because it involves being placed in a tunnel for up to forty-five minutes. This can be an isolating and somewhat claustrophobic experience. Patients with pacemakers, certain clips, and other metal in their bodies cannot undergo this process because of the test's magnetic field.

Thermogram

Muscles that are cramped and tight can raise the temperature of the skin above them, whereas the temperature of the skin over muscles that are chronically inactive may be cool. The thermogram is a test that records heat and is occasionally used to locate painful areas in suspected TMJ patients. It produces a dramatic, high-color, high-tech picture of the pain. The information the thermogram gives may be reliable, but most dentists with an interest in TMJ do not feel that it is necessary for making a diagnosis.

Its one major benefit is that it can help patients confirm that they are feeling pain. It may not tell dentists any more than what they can feel with their fingers, but it does provide a visual aid for a patient and at long last give visible proof that the pain is not in her head!

Tomogram

The tomogram provides a precise and sophisticated view of the jaw joint by taking serial pictures of the joint, slice by slice. Each picture is taken at a slightly different level, allowing the practitioner to view the condyle and temporal bone in great detail. Although tomograms can be a useful diagnostic tool, they do not provide a very good picture of the soft tissues of the joint. It is not possible to view the disc with this method.

Arthrogram and Arthrotomogram

In an *arthrogram*, dye is injected into the jaw joint and X rays are taken of it. The disc, outlined with dye, can then be viewed by a specialist. The *arthrotomogram* also involves injecting dye to outline the jaw joint, but X rays are taken of thin slices of the joint rather than of the whole joint all at once. This makes it more accurate than the arthrogram. The arthrotomogram, because it is sometimes painful and involves radiation, is not commonly used. It has been largely replaced by MRI testing. Less than 5 percent of TMJ patients have arthrotomograms. The test is used, however, if quality MRI is not available nearby or if the patient cannot have an MRI.

Electro-Myographic Study (EMG)

The EMG is used to test the functioning of the facial and neck muscles by monitoring the electric output from the muscles. Little electrodes are placed on the muscles that can sense electricity and transmit it to a machine that makes a printout. A dentist who suspects significant muscle problems and knots might use this test. It can be used both for diagnosis and treatment.

Like other diagnostic tests, some dentists do not find this one useful. They believe that they can get the same information from the physical exam. Palpitating an affected muscle causes pain in the patient, they reason; the EMG is not needed to further document the same pain. EMG remains controversial and its effectiveness has been called into question in recent scientific studies.

CONSERVATIVE TREATMENT AS A DIAGNOSTIC TOOL

Conservative treatment, which is noninvasive and reversible, may be used as a diagnostic tool as well as a treatment. For example, a local anesthesia might be injected into the TMJ joint. If the pain you feel is not relieved by this injection, the pain is probably not TMJ-related. Or a dentist who suspects inflammation of the joint may prescribe conservative treatment for this problem: heat, a soft-food diet, a muscle relaxant, rest, and an antiinflammatory agent such as aspirin. After two to three weeks of this treatment, you would then be reevaluated to see if it helped your pain. If it did, this usually helps to confirm the doctor's original, suspected diagnosis of joint inflammation.

One of the great difficulties in TMJ diagnosis is that a problem originating in the joint can manifest itself as pain in other areas, such as in the head or neck. When the act of biting down hurts, however, the correlation between the pain and the joint is much more obvious.

PAINFUL PRETENDERS

Just as TMJ disorders can mimic other diseases, some serious diseases may look like TMJ disorders. Be on your guard with a doctor who diagnoses you as having TMJ disorder without carefully examining other possibilities. Many, many diseases and medical problems can cause the same symptoms as TMJ disorder.

For example, although headache is often a symptom of TMJ disorder, there are many different types of headaches, and most of them have nothing to do with the TM joint.

Hypertension headaches are caused by high blood pressure. These headaches are usually most severe in the morning. The pain is the generalized, hatband variety. Although a headache caused by TMJ disorder may also be worse in the morning (after a night of clenching or grinding the teeth), high blood pressure is not a symptom of TMJ headaches.

The *migraine* is another important headache type that should not be confused with a TMJ disorder. The migraine is a vascular headache, meaning that it results from the dilation of the blood vessels. The migraine is distinguishable by a group of symptoms: nausea, dizziness, and visual disturbances. It usually strikes only one side of the head and may last anywhere from a few hours to a few days. Most sufferers of migraine are women (the same is true of TMJ disorders). The migraine, however, tends to be inherited, whereas TMJ problems are not.

Menstrual headaches are migrainelike but occur at regular intervals in women during or after the onset of ovulation. TMJ disorders have nothing to do with a woman's monthly cycle.

A *sinus headache* results from a clogged sinus cavity. A clogged sensation in the sinuses is sometimes felt by TMJ sufferers as well, but an MRI or even a simple X ray of the sinuses can show that the TMJ sufferer's sinuses are clear. In this way, the sinus headache can be ruled out.

Temporal arteritis is a serious disorder that can lead to stroke or blindness unless it is treated. This "headache" afflicts women over fifty with a burning or jabbing pain. It is caused by inflamed arteries in the head.

Tic douloureux is rare, but it must not be confused with TMJ disorder because it requires prompt treatment. Tic douloureux is a disease of the neural impulses. The sufferers are mainly women over age fifty-five. Its symptoms include short jabbing pains in the face. TMJ disorder would not cause this type of pain; rather, TMJ pain is usually a dull, nagging ache.

Tumor headaches are also extremely rare but obviously demand immediate attention. Symptoms of brain tumor include headache pain that worsens over time, projectile vomiting, speech and vision disturbances, coordination problems, loss of balance, and seizures.

Other headaches have many other causes, from caffeine withdrawal to hunger to head trauma to eyestrain to arthritis. All these headache types (especially the most medically serious ones) must be ruled out before a diagnosis of TMJ disorder can definitively be made.

A PRECISE DIAGNOSIS

A diagnosis simply of TMJ disorder is not precise enough to be useful. Rather, the specific disorder must be identified: muscle pain, joint inflammation, displaced disc, and so on. A precise diagnosis must be established *before* treatment begins. You should not simply be told that "grinding" is the diagnosis, however. Grinding may be the *reason* for your pain, but it is not a *diagnosis*. The diagnosis would be muscle pain. Understanding the diagnosis is really your first step on the road to recovery. The specialist should explain the diagnosis to you before you go any further. Knowing exactly what your problem is can reduce anxiety and help you get better.

Once the proper diagnosis is made, the prognosis is good. Most people can recover from TMJ disorders and lead pain-free lives. In fact, the treatment is often short and, happily, conservative.

TREATMENT

An accurate diagnosis is only the first step toward relief from TMJ pain's stranglehold on the sufferer's life. The second step is to actually treat the pain. Once the pain has been alleviated, a final step may be to treat the joint problem that caused the pain in the first place, thereby preventing its return. (This, however, is not always necessary.)

As a general rule, treatment for TMJ disorders should always begin with conservative, noninvasive, and reversible therapies. Only very rarely do these noninvasive techniques fail to help, making surgery or other interventions necessary.

Not all cases of TMJ disorder need to be medically treated. The body has an enormous potential to heal itself. Happily, for a large group of people, the symptoms are mild enough to resolve on their own, without any intervention or therapy. Even the classic symptom of clicking in the jaw joint is not necessarily justification for treatment. Clicking, too, may resolve itself with time. If the clicking and popping noises worsen over time, however, treatment would be advisable.

Among those who do undergo treatment, very positive outcomes are being reported. Most dentists who specialize in TMJ disorders believe that about 80 to 85 percent of their patients reach the point where they feel good enough to stop treatment. The pain may not be entirely gone, but it is often 80 percent better, enabling the person to enjoy life again. (This does not always mean, however, that the problem that originally caused the pain has been completely and irreversibly rectified.

Whenever a dentist recommends treatment to you, be sure you understand the diagnosis that underlies the treatment. The dentist should be able to estimate the length of time that will be involved in the treatment and its financial cost. The dentist should answer all your questions honestly and straightforwardly. You must be an active participant in your own care.

Here is a summary of the many possible treatments available to you.

PHYSICAL THERAPY

Physical therapy for the jaw joint is like physical therapy for any other joint in your body. Usually, the patient sees the therapist two to three times a week. Some patients go every day in the beginning, but the visits taper off as the therapy begins to work and patients learn how to care for themselves. Usually, the patient is able to discontinue formal, regular therapy after about three months.

The therapist works with the patient using, among other things, hands-on techniques such as massage, stretching exercises, and strengthening exercises, as well as heat, electrical stimulation, ultrasound, and others. Many of these techniques can be taught to the patient for continued use at home. It is very important that patients learn to continue therapeutic treatment on their own. That way they can help themselves and they will not remain dependent on doctors.

Any patient with a problem that appears to be muscular in origin can be helped by physical therapy and would be referred to a physical therapist. So are patients whom dentists feel have problems that can't be handled with medication, surgery, or dental treatment alone. Almost any TMJ patient can benefit from physical therapy. Physical therapists may even be involved in diagnosis. For example, if a patient mentions to a dentist that her pain is worse when she works at a computer, the dentist may suspect that poor posture and the way the patient holds her head at work may be causing her muscle strain and pain. This patient might then be referred to a physical therapist for further diagnosis.

The main goals of physical therapy for the TMJ patient are:

• to improve function of the jaw

• to relieve pain

• to restore movement

• to prevent reoccurrence of the TMJ disorder

Usually, your dentist will give you the name of a reputable physical therapist. The physical therapist may or may not "specialize" in TMJ disorders. There is no recognized TMJ subspecialty for licensed physical therapists. Still it is probably a good idea to work with a therapist who has some expertise in or a preference for working with TMJ-related problems and injuries.

The role of the physical therapist is extremely important, and your full recovery may hinge on this person's care and your ability to follow through on your own. The therapy is not only of immediate use—in that it can provide relief from pain—but is a preventive measure as well. If a person doesn't learn how to avoid stressing and straining the muscles during routine daily activities, problems with the TM joint will likely recur.

Proper Positioning

A therapist can show you better ways to position your head while you are eating, walking, talking, sleeping, and lifting. Through all these actions, the head should remain in a neutral position. This means that it is held neither forward nor backward of the shoulders.

STANDING. To stand properly, the head is in a neutral position. The earlobe is in direct alignment with the bump on the top of the shoulder. The shoulders are over the hips, and the hips are over the middle arches of the feet. When the head is in a neutral position, muscles are not being put to work. But when the head is out of alignment with the body, the muscles activate and get sore, and muscles that are already sore get even sorer.

LIFTING. Lift objects without straining your neck or gritting your teeth. The head is in the neutral position, and the major work of the lift is done by the leg muscles, not by the neck muscles. Always bend at the knees, not from the waist. While lifting, teeth are not clenched but are instead in a resting position (lips together, tongue at the roof of the mouth, and teeth slightly separated). While lifting, breathe out.

TALKING. The head is in a neutral position. Open and close your mouth properly so that the use of muscles on both sides of your face is symmetrical. If you are talking on the telephone, hold the receiver to your ear. Do not cradle it between your head and shoulder, or your neck muscles will be strained.

EATING. Eat with your head in the neutral position. Do not chew gum. Avoid foods that are tough to chew, like bagels, steaks, heroes, and raw vegetables. Eating soft foods and foods cut into small pieces helps to keep chewing to a minimum and allows the jaw joint to rest.

SLEEPING. Don't sleep on your stomach if your neck is bothering you. Sleep on only one pillow. Inside the pillowcase at the bottom, place a small towel roll. The roll should be right in the curve of your neck under your ears to help keep your head in a neutral position during sleep. Sometimes another simple home treatment is recommended; sleeping on an egg-crate pillow to support the head and neck and reduce muscle stress. An egg-crate pillow is made of foam rubber shaped like an empty egg carton, with peaks and valleys. Your head presses down into the valleys and your neck is supported by the peaks.

WALKING. Hold your head in the neutral position while walking. Do not lead with your head. Wearing rubber-soled, low-heeled shoes can be less jarring to your joints than high heels and work as a shock absorber.

Stretching Exercises

A therapist can help you strengthen weak muscles with exercises and muscle reeducation. Or the therapist can help you stretch a tight muscle to help the jaw open more easily. The stretching may be either gentle or manipulative. For example, your therapist may ask you to open your mouth to a comfortable position, then put your hand in your mouth to stretch it just a bit further. If your jaw deviates to the right on opening, you may be instructed to try to slide the jaw to the left. Then push it a little further with your hand to give it an extra stretch.

It is very important to follow through at home and continue to do the exercises your therapist prescribes. You have to learn what you are doing wrong and how to use your jaw properly.

In addition to positioning and stretching exercises, physical therapists use other techniques as well, including acupressure, behavior modification, biofeedback, ice and heat, isokinetic machines, massage, transcutaneous electrical nerve stimulation (TENS), and ultrasound.

Acupressure

A trained physical therapist can often go right to the trigger point of the problem, where the muscle attaches to the bone. By applying sustained pressure to the area, the therapist can then break up a muscle spasm.

Acupressure works by increasing blood flow to the affected area. The pressure also changes the way the nerve stimulates the muscle so that it can't contract the way it has been, thereby helping to break up the spasm.

A popular spot for acupressure that seems to work well for many TMJ patients is on the coronoid bone of the jaw. This is the bone between the jaw joint and the point where the teeth begin. It is just down from the jaw joint, right under the cheekbone. Pressure on this spot can help to break up a muscle spasm and decrease pain. Your physical therapist can teach you its exact location so that you can use acupressure on it at home.

Behavior Modification

Behavior that causes or aggravates TMJ disorders can be changed. Clenching and grinding the teeth are difficult habits to kick, especially since people often do them unconsciously, while sleeping. Because of this, treatment is directed at preventing the stress that causes the teeth-clenching in the first place. Behavior modification is used to teach a patient better ways to respond to unavoidable stress.

Behavior modification may consist of anything from changing the way a person sleeps to improving their posture to changing the person's reaction to stressful situations. Behavior modification therapy can be given by behavioral therapists or by specialists from other disciplines, such as psychotherapists, psychologists, psychiatrists, and physical therapists. Your regular dentist will refer you to the proper specialist, usually a physical therapist to begin with. This therapist may in turn refer you to someone else for behavior modification, based on your specific needs as well as on the therapist's capabilities. The physical therapist consults with your dentist before referring you to another specialist.

Biofeedback

Biofeedback is a way to control the normally involuntary body functions, including heart rate, blood pressure, and muscle tension. Often in TMJ disorders, a muscle becomes very contracted from the tension of clenched teeth. Biofeedback can be used by the sufferer to relax that muscle.

The process of biofeedback is painless, but it can be time consuming at first. Formal sessions are combined with at-home practice. During the formal sessions, you are hooked up to sophisticated electronic equipment that monitors your body temperature, muscle tension, and heart rate through sensor placed on your skin. You learn to respond to your muscle tension by using relaxation techniques and visual imagery.

Biofeedback can be taught by any number of people: from biofeedback technicians to psychotherapists to psychologists to physical therapists. (For more relaxation tips and ways to reduce stress, see chapter 9.)

Ice and Heat

Ice and heat are both used to relieve the pain of contracted muscles. Cold decreases the activity in the muscle and counters the overstimulation of the muscle. It can also reduce pain by reducing blood flow and swelling. Moist heat is very effective for relieving muscle spasms. Heat increases electrical activity in a muscle and blood flow to the area. This can help to relax the muscle.

Moist heat and moist cold are always suggested. Since both are very effective, the decision between hot and cold is usually made by the preference of the physical therapist or the patient. If one treatment doesn't work, the other one often does.

Isokinetic Machine

The isokinetic machine is used to meet the force of a muscle with equal resistance. It forces the muscle to change in strength and length. It is considered better for building strength than simple weight-lifting exercises because it benefits the entire range of muscle movement and exercises a whole spectrum of muscles.

The isokinetic machine can help strengthen arm and shoulder muscles, which can indirectly help some TMJ patients. Isokinetic machinery is special; it is not likely to be found in a health club. It is usually available only in a physical therapist's office.

Massage

Physical therapists often do massage as well. It may be a gentle, soothing massage to relax the muscles (this feels good) or a much deeper massage to reach the tissues (this does not feel good!). The deep-tissue massage can break up muscle spasm but should be done only by a trained and licensed physical therapist.

Your therapist may perform a transverse friction massage—a deep, concentrated massage done perpendicular to the direction in which the muscle fibers run. That is, if the muscles run horizontally, the massage is done vertically. This type of massage increases the blood flow to the area and decreases inflammation. It can also help speed the healing process.

Transcutaneous Electrical
Nerve Stimulation (TENS)

TENS is a type of electrical stimulation that can be very good for pain relief. The TENS device relieves pain by emitting mild electrical impulses that interfere with and block the pain messages being sent to the brain. The stimulation may be administered either periodically or continuously, depending on need. It may give only temporary relief (perhaps a few hours) and have to be repeated. Most people find that it works best when concentrated on a small area of pain.

TENS can also work to build up a weakened muscle that the patient is unable to move herself. The weakened muscle responds to the electrical stimulation by twitching, which begins to strengthen the muscle.

Ultrasound

Sound waves can be used to penetrate deep into a muscle and relax a muscle spasm. The ultrasound machine converts electrical currents into sound waves that can cause deep heating and break up the spasm. Ultrasound may be used in combination with other treatments or alone. It is repeated several times for best effect.

ORTHODONTICS

Sometimes orthodontics is suggested to correct a bad bite, or malocclusin. A practitioner should substantiate that a bad bite is the problem before suggesting orthodontic work. Unfortunately, the connection between bad bites and TMJ is not well substantiated. If you line up a hundred people without TMJ and a hundred people who suffer from the disorder you'll find an equal number of people with bad bites in each group. A bite plate (a dental appliance) may be used to prevent the upper and lower teeth from coming together and make the pain disappear, but even so, this does not necessarily mean that permanent orthodontic treatment is the proper course of action. Bite plates can also work well on patients with perfect bites!

Occasionally, orthodontic treatment should be considered. Ultimately, you want the best bite possible to support the jaw joint effectively. Do not allow someone to start grinding your teeth down to improve your bite, however. This is an irreversible commonly misguided treatment. If this treatment is suggested to you, get other opinions before agreeing. (For more on orthodonture, see "Permanent Improvements," below.)

Bite Plates

A bite plate (also known as a *splint*, a *night guard*, an *occlusal appliance*, and an *orthotic*) is a piece of clear plastic that slips on over the teeth to keep them from closing all the way. It is somewhat similar in design to a retainer.

The bite plate helps both jaw-joint and jaw-muscle problems, it is believed, by opening up the bite and preventing the teeth from coming together. If the teeth don't meet, the ball of the joint doesn't compress into the socket. This takes pressure off the joint and gives an inflamed joint a chance to rest. Moreover, opening the bite also relieves pressure on the bones, the joint, and the tissues, so that the muscles that close the jaw are rested. This can also help the facial muscles to relax.

Bite plates control the grinding and clenching that can lead to TMJ disorders. The person wearing a bite plate may still grind her teeth, but she is now grinding on the plate; the teeth themselves are protected. If a person has an uneven bite, the plate can compensate for this and make the bite more even.

Although it is a very successful therapy, not every patient with a TMJ disorder will get a bite plate. A good dentist listens, reviews, and checks for a myriad of problems before deciding to try a bite plate. In general, a bite plate is considered a conservative treatment, but some types are more invasive than others.

You should be aware of the differences among bite plates. No one argues with the fact that bite plates work well for many people. But everyone argues about *which type* of bite plate works best. Available types of bite plates include: upper plates, lower plates, hard plates, soft plates, plates that cover all the teeth, plates that cover only a few teeth, plates that are flat, and plates that are made to push the jaw into a new position. Let's look at the choices.

UPPER VERSUS LOWER BITE PLATE. There seems to be no difference between the two. One person may find the lower bite plate more comfortable; another may find the upper more comfortable. If you have to wear it all day, you may find that talking is easier when wearing a lower plate.

HARD VERSUS SOFT BITE PLATE. Plates can be made from hard or soft materials. The hard plates may be better for long-term use. The soft plates tend to deteriorate over time.

ALL TEETH COVERED VERSUS SOME TEETH COVERED. The bite plate that covers all the teeth is preferable for long-term use. A bite plate that covers only some of the teeth may have an orthodontic effect if used over a long period of time—that is, it can change your bite. On the other hand, the benefits of partial coverage are that it is easier to talk and is more comfortable for the wearer.

FLAT VERSUS MANIPULATIVE PLATES. In keeping with the philosophy of conservative treatment, it is better to use a bite plate that does *not* reposition the jaw. Only a handful of people need to have their jaws repositioned. A manipulative plate makes it necessary to eventually cap all the teeth or to get braces. If a manipulative plate is suggested to you, get second and third opinions before proceeding. Find out how long you would be expected to wear one. Manipulative plates are meant for short-term use only.

One reason there are so many varied opinions about the merits of different bite-plate types is that no one really knows why bite plates work as well as they do.

A dentist ordering a bite plate will custom-make it to fit your mouth and your situation. After the initial fitting, the plate will need some fine tuning; you will have to return to the dentist's office so that the plate can be ground down for an even bite. Several follow-up visits may be necessary to get it perfect. A bite plate may be worn all the time or some of the time. Some are worn all day but must be removed to eat. Others are worn only during the night. Some patients are given one type of bite plate for daytime use and another type for nighttime wear.

At first, it may be hard to get used to the plate. It will feel odd and uncomfortable and may interfere with your speech until you grow accustomed to it. After a week or two, the bite plate will be like an old friend! You will adjust to it so well that taking it out may eventually feel uncomfortable.

Depending on the design, some bite plates are more cosmetically appealing than others. Some bite plates cannot readily be noticed on the wearer; others are more obvious. There are ways to make a bite plate unobtrusive, however. It can be trimmed back so that it covers only about one-quarter inch of the front teeth. The part that does show is, like the rest of the plate, made of clear plastic. Basically, the bite plate is made to cover the biting surfaces of the teeth—an area that does not readily show. Many patients wear these plates all day—to business meetings, before juries in court, to social events—without any embarrassment about their looks.

No matter what the design, however, all bite plates interfere somewhat with speech patterns. Some people experience few if any problems with their speech and adjust easily to the bite plate. Others find that the plate interferes a great deal with their ability to speak, and these people must remove the plate to speak at business meetings or on the telephone. With use, however, most people adjust to the bite plate and soon have much less difficulty speaking with it in place. Much depends on the particular person's agility in speech.

A bite plate should be worn until the patient feels that it is no longer needed. A plate may resolve the problem in as few as two to three weeks. A bite plate worn to take pressure off an inflamed joint can allow the joint to heal in a matter of weeks. A bite plate worn for a grinding or clenching problem, however, may need to be worn for a much longer period of time. Often, daytime wear is phased out but night wear continues. The length of time a bite plate is needed varies from person to person and treatment to treatment. Much depends on the type of problem you have and how quickly your particular body is able to heal.

TRIGGER POINT INJECTIONS

In severe cases of TMJ disorder, a dentist may suggest administering a trigger point injection. Usually, this injection is of an anesthetic like xylocaine. Xylocaine has no real side effects, although like any drug, it is always very slightly possible that someone will be allergic to it. An occasional patient also reacts nervously to shots and faints. In rare cases, the injection site is sore for twenty-four hours afterward, but this disappears.

Anesthetic injections numb the affected muscles. Pain relief may last for a few days or a few weeks. After the pain relief diminishes, the injection is repeated. The therapy breaks up the muscle spasm and gives the muscle time to heal. As the muscle improves, the patient is able to go longer between injections, until finally they are no longer necessary.

Some dentists inject steroids instead of anesthetics. Steroid injections can dramatically reduce inflammation. Although one-to-two steroid injections are okay, repeated injections are not advisable and can lead to problems, such as muscle necrosis. In muscle necrosis, scar tissue that inhibits muscle movement forms.

NUTRITION

The jaw, like any other part of the body, depends on good nutrition for good health. Healthy muscles and bones heal more quickly and are less likely to be reinjured. Some people believe that vitamins can be used therapeutically to heal TMJ disorders. There is no scientific evidence to support this view, however.

TMJ patients may want to cut down on caffeine. Caffeine is a stimulant that can increase muscle tension and make you more sensitive to pain.

It may be unwise to follow only a nutritional therapy to the exclusion of more conventional therapies.

SOFT-FOOD DIET

Sometimes a diet of soft food is suggested to give the jaw a chance to rest and heal. The diet is followed for a few weeks to allow time for the inflammation to die down. In extremely severe cases, when jaws simply cannot open, a liquid diet may be suggested. After open-joint surgery, a liquid or soft diet is necessary for a few weeks, allowing for recovery time. In less severe, nonsurgical cases, however, restraint may be suggested and nutritional guidelines may be given to help rest the jaws.

Foods to Avoid

- nuts

- large slices or chunks of raw vegetables

- hard candies

- hard rolls

- chewing gum

- steaks and other chewy meats
- apples
- caramels and other sticky foods

Foods to Try

- pasta
- minced or shredded fresh vegetables
- cooked vegetables
- cooked fruit
- soup
- hash
- mashed potatoes
- chopped or minced meat
- casseroles
- pudding, custard, ice cream

MEDICATION AND DRUG ADDICTION

If you suffered from TMJ disorder for months or years before receiving proper diagnosis and treatment, you may have taken numerous over-the-counter pain killers in an attempt to alleviate your pain. One possible side effect is addiction to these medications.

Unfortunately, drugs have always been a very popular

method of treatment. In the past, patients were routinely given Valium and muscle relaxants. Today, such drugs are still prescribed but with greater selectivity.

Each patient must make the very personal decision about whether he or she feels comfortable with drug therapy. Many people prefer to explore other avenues before they take medications. Others, however, make drug therapy their personal first choice for treatment. Although some people—and their doctors—feel that the risk of abuse and addiction with drugs like Valium is too high, others feel that the benefits can outweigh the risks. The bottom line is that drugs, if properly prescribed and taken in small doses, can be beneficial to some patients.

Medications that are currently being prescribed for TMJ disorders include:

Antiinflammatory Drugs

Aspirin is an antiinflammatory drug; many others are available by prescription only. A dentist may prescribe Naprosyn, Clinoril, Dolobid, Motrin, or Trilisate, all of which work to reduce swelling and inflammation in the jaw joint.

Muscle Relaxants

Muscle relaxants may be prescribed for patients with unusually tight muscles. They can be especially effective when nighttime grinding and clenching are part of the problem. Common brand names include Flexeril, Robaxin, and Soma.

Antianxiety Drugs

Valium is perhaps the best-known drug for the relief of anxiety. Others include Xanax and Ativan. Anxiety can be a major culprit in TMJ disorders that are caused by tight muscles. Other ways of curbing anxiety include exercise, biofeedback, and psychiatric therapy. Drugs may not be the preferred method in this case. Antianxiety medications can also act as muscle relaxants.

Antidepressants

Occasionally, a patient needs a prescription for an antidepressant, a medication that works to reduce depression and kill pain. Antidepressants can be effective for patients suffering from debilitating chronic pain and the resulting depression. Medications such as Elavil, Pamelor, and Prozac help the body produce natural pain killers.

Any of these medications may be suggested to you as a treatment or in conjunction with other methods of treatment. You may have strong personal opinions about taking drugs for a health problem. Talk with your dentist to find out which are necessary and which are optional.

Medications should not be taken over long periods of time, or dependency can build. Usually TMJ patients are offered a medication for no more than a few months.

Each drug has many advantages and some disadvantages. One major advantage is that the proper drugs used at the right time can help to speed recovery. They can give the body a head start on the healing process. Ask your doctor to explain the benefits, risks, and side effects of any drug prescribed. Only then will you be able to make a rational decision about its use.

PERMANENT IMPROVEMENTS

After the pain has been taken care of and the patient begins to resume a normal life, more permanent improvements can be made to prevent the problem from recurring. Permanent changes, however, are only rarely indicated.

For some people, the TMJ disorder remains after the symptoms are relieved. For example, consider a TMJ sufferer who has a disc out of place. After three months of treatment with a soft-food diet, a bite plate, and mild exercise, the pain diminishes and the symptoms lessen. Although the person is no longer suffering, the underlying problem remains: the disc is still out of place. Should a permanent improvement be made now?

Most dentists would say no. The usual goals of TMJ therapy are pain relief and normal jaw use. Once they have been achieved, therapy is usually concluded and permanent improvements are not made.

Occasionally, however, a patient *can* benefit from such intervention. If, for example, a patient's pain is relieved by a bite plate but the patient remains totally dependent upon the appliance for pain relief, this may signal the need for more drastic, nonreversible therapy. The patient may not want to live the rest of her life totally dependent on the plate. The practitioner may then suggest going beyond the conservative and reversible techniques that were first used to treat the pain.

If nonreversible treatment is suggested to you, find out why. Keep in mind that permanent improvements are not usually necessary. If your pain has disappeared, you may not need to go any further.

For those who need permanent improvements, the following techniques are considered:

Equilibration

Equilibration is a dental method used to balance an uneven bite. The dentist grinds and smooths the surfaces of the teeth to make sure no high spots are throwing your bite off balance. Sometimes, even small irregularities can affect normal jaw movements and fatigue the muscles. Always get a second opinion before allowing a dentist to grind your teeth. This treatment is often overused.

Onlays

Onlays are used for teeth that have been worn down and need to be built back up. An onlay is usually made of gold or porcelain. Porcelain onlays are laminated onto the biting surface of the teeth. Because of its color and material, it blends in well with the natural look of your teeth, and the restorative work is not noticeable. Gold is still sometimes used, however, in areas of low visibility because it provides such a durable biting surface.

Crowns and Caps

A crown or cap may be the answer for a tooth that cannot be restored with an onlay. Sometimes there just isn't enough tooth left to hold the onlay, and so a crown is used instead. A crown or cap covers the entire area above the gum where the original tooth used to be. The original tooth's roots and ligaments are still attached.

False Teeth

False teeth may be the answer for people with many missing teeth. Missing teeth can affect and throw off the balance of a bite. A false tooth can usually be attached to the other teeth in your mouth, using a *bridge*.

For a bridge, the two teeth on either side of the missing tooth are ground down and capped. A dummy tooth is then placed in the middle and fixed to the capped teeth. This false tooth is not removable.

If a lot of teeth are missing, a bridge is impossible. *Dentures* may be the only answer. There are partial dentures and full dentures. Full dentures are used when there are no teeth left. They replace everything—they cover the gum and rest on top of the gum. They are removable. Adhesive may be necessary to hold full dentures in place, but if the patient's gums are in good condition, they will stay in place without adhesive. If some good teeth remain, partial dentures can be used instead. These clip onto the remaining healthy teeth. Partial dentures, like full dentures, are removable.

Implants

Implants may be used to fill in the spaces where teeth are missing. Although this method is appealing because implants provide permanent and nonremovable false teeth, dentists do not consider implants to be a first choice in most cases. Implants are not for everyone. First of all, only people with very good supportive bone structure can be considered for implants. Second, once the implants are in place, oral hygiene must be scrupulous. (This can be a lot to expect of a person who may have lost his natural teeth due to poor hygiene in the first place.) The patient must take excellent care of these dummy teeth because if an implant is lost, there will be partial bone loss as well. Furthermore, the TMJ patients are often poor candidates for implants because they are often clenchers and grinders. Teeth grinding can put too much stress on implants.

Braces

Braces can straighten teeth and push them back into their correct original position. It is not merely a cosmetic procedure; orthodontic work may be necessary for the patient who has had a manipulative splint in his mouth. This type of splint changes your bite, and the new bite often must be stabilized by orthodonture. It can take years to undergo orthodontic work. The force that moves your teeth must be applied slowly.

Today's braces no longer look much like the "railroad tracks" of your childhood memories. Instead of metal bands, brackets are now bonded to the tooth surfaces. Sometimes plastic brackets and wires are used instead of steel. There are even braces that appear on the back sides of teeth, but these are not suitable for all cases.

Before proceeding with any of these permanent methods of restorative dentistry, make sure you get a second opinion. These are, after all, irreversible measures that change the bite and movement of the jaw. Always ask, as well, whether there are risks involved: Can the procedure do any harm?

SEVEN

SURGERY—
THE FINAL FRONTIER

Occasionally, surgery on the joint should be considered. Although any type of surgery is regarded as a "last resort" treatment, sometimes surgery offers the best chance of recovery from the debilitating effects of TMJ disorder. Surgery may be combined with orthodontics to move the jaw into a better position and to develop a better bite. Recovery from surgery can be quick, which may prove to be preferable to years of ongoing conservative treatment.

Happily, only about 5 to 10 percent of TMJ sufferers have symptoms that are disabling enough to possibly warrant surgery. Of these sufferers, not all choose surgery. Some do so well with nonsurgical treatment that TMJ surgery is no longer warranted.

Some of the physical conditions that may necessitate surgery are:

- dislocation of the articular disc
- osteoarthritis in the joint
- structural defects in the bones of the jaws
- a torn or perforated disc

QUALIFICATIONS FOR SURGERY

There are four main qualifications for surgical treatment:

Pain

Severe pain may indicate the need for surgery. Unfortunately, it is very difficult to measure the level and intensity of a person's pain. A dentist must rely on the patient's perception and description of that pain. Only the patient can determine how much pain she is in and how it affects the quality of her life.

Dysfunction

One strong indicator of the need for surgical treatment is when a jaw simply can't open to a reasonable width. In a severe TMJ disorder, the disc gets stuck in front of the joint and causes the jaw to lock. The jaw simply won't open past a certain point. The person can't chew properly, brush her teeth, or open wide enough to talk without trouble. The dentist can measure the space between the open jaws, but only the patient can say how the jaw-locking affects her life.

One female patient whose jaw opens only to 8 mm instead of the normal 35–50 mm has decided against surgery. She has been able to cope with her affliction well enough in her own life that she feels surgery is not currently necessary. She has a husband, children, a good job, and a satisfying quality of life.

Failed Conservative Treatment

After three to six months of conservative treatment that has *not* benefited the patient, surgery may become an option.

Repairable Damage

The question is, Will surgery fix the problem? If a disc is out of place or if the connective tissues have ripped or torn, surgery may be a solution. Surgery can often repair the joint. In some cases, the joint can even be removed and replaced.

BEFORE SURGERY

Before you undergo any surgery, a complete health history will be taken. You will undergo a blood test, X rays, a urine test, and a complete physical. If your surgery is to be performed under general anesthesia, you should meet with the anesthesiologist. All these precautions are taken to make sure that you don't suffer from any condition that makes surgery inadvisable.

Any surgery involving the face is done with great care. The surgical incision is made at the same spot where incisions for face-lifts are always made—at the crease by the ears. All surgical incisions leave scars, but the minor scarring from this operation does not show much due to the location of the incision. Your hair will not be shaved for the operation. Sometimes a small portion of hair at the hairline is shaved, but enough hair always remains to cover the shaved spot later.

Because the head must be kept immobile during joint surgery, general anesthesia is almost always used.

TYPES OF SURGERY

Great strides have been made in the use of surgery for TMJ disorders. Patients and doctors now have several options and can choose from among more- and less-invasive techniques.

Arthroscopic Surgery

Once done only on knee joints, arthroscopic surgery is now being used on jaw joints. This is a new and exciting breakthrough for TMJ sufferers because arthroscopic surgery is quicker, cheaper, less painful, and less intrusive than previous forms of joint surgery. Even so, arthroscopic surgery should not be done unless it is justified and all nonsurgical remedies have failed. Surgery—of no matter what type—should be considered only when no other treatment options exist.

Arthroscopy is usually done under general anesthesia in a hospital setting. The patient needn't be admitted, however, and can leave the hospital the same day. An arthroscope is essentially a miniature microscope the size of a large needle. It is used to see into the joint. Using a set of canulas (hollow tubes with sharp, needle-like points at the end), the oral and maxillofacial surgeon perforates the joint from the outside. The puncture is small, requires no stitching, and leaves only a pin-point scar. The dental surgeon places the arthroscope through the canula. Once the arthroscope is in place in the joint, a picture of the joint is displayed on a TV screen. The picture is detailed and in full color and enables the surgeon to get a good look at the joint structures.

The surgeon can check the position of the disc, the nature of the joint inflammation, and the presence of scar tissue. He or she can gauge any joint degeneration, look at the ligaments holding the disc (are they stretching or tearing?), check for joint disease, and observe how the condyles move by opening and closing the patient's mouth. This is the diagnostic portion of arthroscopic surgery. Treatment can also be provided: inflamed areas may be shaved away; scar bands (adhesions) can be broken up (lysed); or a laser may be used to treat scarring. Because the tools used are so tiny and the work space is so small, the surgeon is obviously somewhat limited. For this reason, open joint surgery, though much more invasive, remains a necessary option for some patients.

Interestingly, arthroscopy itself seems to have therapeutic value. In order to perform the arthroscopy, a fluid is continuously pumped through the joint to keep the image clear. This constant flushing and lavaging of the joint seems to provide relief for many patients.

Postsurgical recovery is quick. The patient leaves the hospital the same day, with a bandage. There may be some swelling or tenderness at the site of the operation, but this disappears in day or two.

Open Joint Surgery

Although it is more intrusive, open joint surgery is necessary in certain situations. In open joint surgery, an incision is made just in front of the ear. The incision is usually less than two inches long, and its location makes any resulting scar relatively unnoticeable. In open joint surgery, the surgeon may sew, shave bone, or even take the disc out and replace it. A joint replacement might be dictated in the case of severe arthritis.

Disc plication is a common type of TMJ surgery, used when the disc has slipped off the condyle. During the disc plication operation, the disc is pulled back into place and sewn there. This type of surgery has met with much success.

Open joint surgery may take a couple of hours, and recovery time is longer than with arthroscopy. The area may be tender for a few days. Sometimes antiinflammatory drugs are prescribed postsurgically. A soft diet is suggested for up to three weeks to give the joint time to heal. Physical therapy is then begun. Physical therapy is always important after an operation because it can reduce scar tissue and prevent stiffness in the joint from developing.

Orthognathic Surgery

Orthognathic surgery is more invasive and more serious. It is used to correct severe jaw problems involving bone defects, such as a mandible that is too large or too small or bones that are asymmetrical—larger on one side of the face than the other. If a condition is so severe that it cannot be helped by orthodontics, splints, or other surgical procedures, orthognathic surgery can be used to reposition and reshape the bones of the jaw. The mandible can actually be shortened or lengthened. Like open joint surgery, orthognathic surgery carries a risk of facial numbness, which, though it is rare, should be told to you. After the surgery, the jaws may need to be wired together to prevent movement. A liquid or soft-food diet would be given during this recovery period.

QUESTIONS TO ASK BEFORE YOU UNDERGO SURGERY

- What risks are involved in arthroscopic surgery? (Damage to a nerve or blood vessel is possible but rare.) What risks are involved in open joint surgery?

- Is there a chance that complications would cause the surgeon to switch from arthroscopy to open joint surgery?

- What risks are involved in general anesthesia?

- What types of lab tests, X rays, and medications are usually necessary in connection with this surgery?

- May I see the consent form I will have to sign?

- How long does the operation take?

- How much does the hospital charge (beyond what the surgeon charges)

- How soon may I leave the hospital?

- What type of postsurgical treatment will I need (medications, physical therapy, restricted diet)?

- What are my chances for a good recovery?

- How soon can I resume my normal activities?

FINDING THE RIGHT SURGEON

To find an oral and maxillofacial surgeon, try these methods:

- Ask your general dentist for a referral.

- Call the American Association of Oral and Maxillofacial Surgeons (1-800-822-6637) and ask for the name of a board-certified surgeon in your area.

- Call a dental school, if there is one near you. Ask for the department of oral and maxillofacial surgery, and get some names from them.

- Call a major medical center and ask for the department of oral and maxillofacial surgery. They will be able to tell you some names.

- Contact a TMJ clinic.

- Your local dental society may be able to refer you to a good surgeon. If not, try the American Dental Association (1-800-621-8099) and ask for names of board-certified oral and maxillofacial surgeons in your area.

Once you have a name or two, arrange for a consultation with them. When consulting with a surgeon, you may want to ask the following questions:

- Are you an oral and maxillofacial surgeon?

- Are you board certified by the American Board of Oral and Maxillofacial Surgery? (Do not use a surgeon who is not board certified.)

- How often do you perform this operation? (It is advisable to use a surgeon who does this type of surgery regularly.)

- Where did you receive your training? (The answer may be of some interest to you, but as long as the surgeon is board certified, it should not be of major importance.)

- How long have you been in practice?

- What is your success rate in cases like mine? (Different surgeons can have different success rates with the same operation. You will want to choose a surgeon who seems best able to perform the operation successfully. Beware, however, of someone who says they have a 100 percent success rate! You should also bear in mind that the success rate of any surgery is related not only to the ability of the surgeon but also to the nature of the particular problem.)

- How much do you charge for this surgery? (Check with your insurance company to determine if this fee will be covered. Depending on the amount of pain and severity of the problem, you may choose to proceed even if the cost is not covered by your insurance.)

• You should ask specific questions that are important to you: Why is the surgery necessary? How long will it take to recover from the surgery? What kind of improvement can I expect?

After you have met with a surgeon, you will have to decide whether he or she is the right one for you.

• Did you feel comfortable with this surgeon?

• Did you like the way your questions were answered? Are you satisfied with the answers?

• Was the surgeon willing to answer all your questions, or was he or she defensive about the questions?

• Was the office well run or disorganized? Friendly or cold?

• Did you like the surgeon's support staff? (You will have to deal with these people to make appointments, discuss billing and insurance claims, and the like.)

• What reputation does the hospital have?

A WORD ABOUT INSURANCE

Always check your dental and medical insurance policies to find out how you are covered. Oral and maxillofacial surgery is usually covered by medical policies. Fees for

TMJ surgery are most often recoverable. Not all insurance companies cover TMJ-related treatments, however, and you should find out which treatments are allowed and which are excluded before you try to file a claim.

EIGHT

COPING WITH PAIN

The pain of TMJ disorders, coupled with the difficulty that is sometimes involved in finding the cause of that pain, presents a very difficult situation for most sufferers. By the time they arrive at TMJ clinics or dentists' offices, many are almost out of hope. They may fear that the pain that has plagued them for months or even years will never go away.

Once a diagnosis of TMJ disorder has been made and treatment is under way, however, the patient's sense of relief is great. At last, there is a *reason* for the pain and a way to escape from it. At last, plans can be made for the future without the specter of pain looming over every decision.

Unfortunately, many misconceptions exist about people who suffer from pain as TMJ patients do. People may think you are making it up to get attention or to get out of work. A spouse may believe that you are using the pain as a way to say you are unhappy with the relationship or that you are trying to control the marriage through it.

When you live with pain that won't go away, you must find ways to keep it from ruining your life. By reading this book and getting to the bottom of your painful condition, you are taking an important step in the right direction.

CHRONIC PAIN PATIENTS

The depression and anxiety that chronic pain patients feel can contribute to their pain. It becomes a vicious cycle: pain leads to depression; depression lowers the pain threshold; the pain gets worse; then the depression over the pain gets worse.

Some patients who have suffered from chronic pain for years are very difficult to treat. This may be partly because for them, pain has become a way of life. Although it sounds odd, some therapists believe that chronic pain patients occasionally reach a point where giving up their pain is too hard. It would mean a whole new life—change and readjustment. Such a person needs to see a therapist or psychiatrist before other treatment can be of help.

THE EFFECT ON THE FAMILY

Unfortunately, pain that affects you affects your family as well. The demands you make on them may be great; medical bills may be an added burden. As sympathetic as spouses and family members are, they cannot share the pain. And when pain goes on for a long time their sympathy may run out and be replaced by more selfish thoughts. This is human nature, not vindictiveness.

To keep your family life on an even keel, try to do some of these things:

- Show an interest in the lives of your family members. Ask about their day. Let them know you care. They may be feeling left alone, as if your pain were stealing the whole show.

- Try to keep your complaints to a minimum.

- Do not expect children to understand your situation. Young children tend to be very egocentric and see only how things affect *them.*

- Be straightforward with your spouse if you need help with the daily tasks of life. If he knows what you need, he'll be better able to accommodate you.

- Consider getting someone to help you around the house—with gardening, housekeeping, or child care.

- Involve your spouse in the positive side of your treatment. Let him know of improvements as you start to feel better. Ask if he would like to help you with your relaxation exercises or do the massage the physical therapist has taught you.

- Get psychiatric help if you need it. Do not be embarrassed about getting this help. Ask your doctor or dentist for a referral. It may help to talk things out with a professional. It's also possible that psychotherapy can alleviate your pain by ending some of the mental stress that may be causing it.

STRESS REDUCERS

It is important for TMJ sufferers to learn how to deal effectively with the daily stresses of life. Relaxation exercises and stress reducers are of particular value to patients whose TMJ disorders resulted from their tension. Clenching and grinding the teeth, for example, are often nervous habits used as a coping mechanism.

Here are some ways to help to reduce the stress in your life.

• When tension strikes, breathe deeply. Inhale through your nose, and exhale—slowly—through your mouth. Repeat until you begin to feel the tension dissipate.

• Try to relax all the muscles in your body. Concentrate on the muscles of the face and neck. "Talk" to these muscles so that you can purposely relax each one. It may help to say, "Relax your jaw," "Relax your shoulders," and so on, letting each part you call out droop.

• Use mental imagery to give yourself a break from the rigors of the day. A short daydream about sitting by a pool or fishing for trout is as good as a minivacation!

• Leave yourself plenty of time for life's unexpected hassles. Get up earlier in the morning, or set out sooner for appointments. When you are less rushed, you are less tense.

• Keep a calendar handy. Don't rely on your memory for everything.

• Don't let long lines set your teeth a-gnashing. Carry a magazine to read if you have to wait.

- Find out what aggravates you most, and make a change for the better. Does that creaky door set your teeth on edge? Oil it! Is your car a constant source of worry and frustration? Trade it in for a new one!

- Relax your standards. Perfection is not only unattainable but can be detrimental to your health. The world will not end if you attack certain tasks with less vigor than you have been.

- Learn to say no. Do not crowd your days with countless appointments, projects, and promises to do more.

- Keep a journal, and vent your feelings there. This is also a good place to complain freely about TMJ problems without burdening a family member.

- Take a leisurely bath to soak tension away.

- Relax on the weekends. Do not use them to rearrange the house or to catch up on office work.

Every life has stresses built in. Learn to live with these; go with the flow. When you are better able to handle daily tension, you are less likely to wear your teeth and stress your jaw joint with nervous clenching and grinding. Take time out to practice a little healthy relaxation. Your jaw joint will thank you for it.

REBUILDING YOUR LIFE

Once they are pain free, many patients must set about rebuilding their lives, their careers, and their marriages. For example, they can resume the sports activities they once enjoyed but had to give up due to the chronic pain.

This return to the athletic life can provide someone who loves sports with a renewed sense of self and more energy. At last, you feel healthy and whole again! Remember, though, to reenter an athletic life with care and common sense. You don't want to retrigger a jaw problem by doing too much too soon. Muscles that have been stressed or that were in spasms may still be more sensitive to damage.

Patients who have been on soft-food diets can slowly return to normal foods. Again, use some caution and restraint. Your dentist will give you guidelines.

After successful TMJ treatment, patients sleep better and eat better and have a new outlook on life. Most report a renewed sense of vigor after treatment. The constant pain they experienced before was an undeniable energy drain. Enjoyment of life returns, as does a satisfying sex life. (It can often be difficult to maintain a happy sex life in the face of pain.)

Other health problems can also be addressed after TMJ disorder has been dealt with. Exercise and weight-loss programs can at last be joined. Headaches and problems unrelated to TMJ disorder can now be singled out and dealt with. This is a time to get your life back in order.

FUTURE DENTAL CARE

Soon you will return to a normal life and see your dentist only for routine cleanings and cavities. If you start seeing a new dentist, make sure he or she is aware of your TMJ history. To provide you with the safest and best dental care, your dentist will need to know exactly what treatments you underwent and what problems were resolved. Occasionally, dental work brings TMJ symptoms back, but this is not likely, especially if the work is done by someone sensitive to the delicate balance now in your mouth.

NINE

A FEW
CASE HISTORIES

It may help you to hear about the stories of others like you—people who suffered from TMJ pain, who sought help and found relief. (Although based on true stories, the names of the patients and other details of their cases have been changed.)

LOVE AT FIRST BITE

Marybeth was a troubled woman. It was hard for her to remember a time when pain did not plague her. After suffering through twelve years of recurring headaches, she had slowly become convinced that the pain was all in her head and that she was simply neurotic. She had seen a number of doctors for her headaches and had tried numerous physical treatments, but none had helped. Finally, she had turned to psychiatric therapy. One specialist reminded her that her headaches had begun at the time of her father's death. This convinced her that her pain had no physical basis. Yet although she remained in therapy, there was still no resolution to her pain.

Fortunately, Marybeth began to date a young dental student. By the time they married, he was a practicing dentist with a budding interest in disorders of the temporomandibular joint. Familiar with his bride's complaints and her search for relief from pain, he explored the possibility that she was a victim of a TMJ disorder. He brought her into his office and made a bite plate for her to allow her jaw to rest. Within two weeks, her headaches had disappeared.

For Marybeth, it was a miracle. Years of suffering at last came to an end. Today, she is pain free and no longer wears a bite plate. Her husband now helps many others like her who suffer from TMJ disorders.

GETTING TO THE TOOTH OF THE MATTER

After reading about TMJ disorders in magazines and newspapers, Joanne began to suspect that she might be a TMJ sufferer since she was experiencing muscle pain in the jaw area. She made an appointment at a well-respected university clinic, and when she arrived, the dentist began by asking her for a complete medical and dental history. He asked her to describe the pain she felt and its location. Her pain, she indicated, emanated both from a tooth and from her jaw. The dentist proceeded to test her range of jaw motion, which seemed normal. He palpated the muscles of the jaw and found no pain or pressure to the joint or muscle.

During the comprehensive and thorough diagnostic period that followed, the TMJ experts began to suspect that her muscle pain had nothing to do with her temporomandibular joint. They ordered an X ray of her teeth, and there in black and white lay the deceptively simple answer: Her problem and her pain stemmed from a tooth. She needed root-canal work. Due to the pain from this one tooth, she had stopped biting there, which had been causing muscle strain in the jaw. The root-canal work was promptly done, and in no time her muscle pain disappeared almost completely.

A DISC IN TIME

A forty-six-year-old female office manager suffered for almost ten years from chronic pain after she was in an auto accident. She described the pain as feeling "as if the top of my head were on fire." During her decade of pain, she saw many different specialists but was unable to find relief. Finally, she went to see a dentist, and TMJ disorder was diagnosed. Her treatment involved a bite plate, biofeedback, and psychological and physical therapy. A slipped disc in her neck was also found. She now avoids foods that might injure her jaw and continues to wear her bite plate during certain stressful times. Happily, her pain has disappeared, and she now leads a normal life.

THE LONG
AND WINDING ROAD

As a teenager, Linda had been a promising young athlete. She had played field hockey and ran track. Unfortunately, a fall during her high school years put an end to her athletic career. She began to suffer from headaches and from neck and back pain that would not go away. She received chiropractic treatment and physical therapy in the hope that she would find a remedy and be able to return to the sports she loved, but she couldn't get much relief from the pain.

Eleven years later, still suffering from headaches, she was at last diagnosed as having a TMJ disorder. A bite plate was made for her, and physical therapy was begun; within 5 months, her symptoms began to disappear. Although she still feels some pain, the quality of her life is much improved. She continues to wear the bite plate, but only when she is under stress. Her reliance on physical therapy is decreasing. She is thinking about taking up jogging and wants to slowly return to physical activities.

ASPIRIN FREE

Jim, a forty-four-year-old man in the insurance business, made an appointment with his regular dentist. He was experiencing mouth pain and wanted to know what was wrong. His dentist performed the typical dental exam and took X rays but was baffled—he could find no cause for Jim's pain. It seemed that nothing could be done about the pain. Jim hoped that it would simply disappear with time.

Soon, however, Jim's problems escalated. He experienced earaches, toothaches, and headaches, and the pain on the left side of his jaw began to increase. His dependency on aspirin was also increasing. With mounting concern, Jim contacted an oral surgeon who had been suggested to him by his dentist.

The oral surgeon listened to Jim's complaints and examined him. He finally suggested that his problem might be TMJ related. He suggested that Jim go ahead with some conservative treatment for TMJ disorder in the hope that it would solve the problem. Jim agreed. After treatment with a bite plate and exercises suggested by a physical therapist, the pain completely disappeared. He hasn't used any aspirin since treatment for TMJ disorder began.

GRINDING TO A HALT

Christina was no stranger to dental pain. A thirty-year-old woman, she frequently complained to her friends and family about her aching jaws and periodic headaches. An avid gum chewer and teeth grinder, she had been experiencing intermittent pain for ten years but had learned to live with it. Her discomfort had not kept her from pursuing a successful career as a real estate agent or from marrying and having two children during those years.

But then more severe pain attacks began. She got shooting pains from jaw to temple. She got headaches and blurred vision. She was checked for diabetes, glaucoma, and even for brain tumor; she underwent numerous diagnostic tests, including an EKG, an EEG, X rays, and CAT scan. No cause for her pain could be discovered. She saw a dentist and had her wisdom teeth removed. Still there was no improvement. She eventually tried tranquilizers and psychotherapy—all to no avail.

Finally, Christina saw a dentist who had a special interest in TMJ. He listened with interest as she described herself as a teeth grinder and gum chewer. He looked over her medical history and saw that many possible diagnoses had been ruled out. He made her a bite plate to ease the tension from her grinding.

With the help of the bite plate, Christina stopped grinding her teeth. She uses biofeedback to help relax and to curb her headaches. She underwent physical therapy to relax and strengthen her muscles.

Now she says, "My attitude has changed. I actually laugh and smile every day. I look forward to the rest of my life—something I never thought I would hear myself say."

A SURGICAL ANSWER

Sixteen-year-old Amy sat in a dentist's chair and complained of difficulty in opening her mouth due to pain. The dentist's examination showed clearly that the range of her jaw movements was diminished due to her pain. Suspecting a TMJ disorder, he began six months of conservative treatment, including bite plates and physical therapy. Everyone expected that this would be enough, but Amy's pain did not go away.

After some discussion, Amy was referred to and met with an oral and maxillofacial surgeon. His examination led him to suggest surgery. This suggestion was then discussed with Amy's dentist. After questioning him about possible scarring, side effects, and success rates, Amy and her family agreed to the operation. Arthroscopy was performed. During the surgery, a displaced disc was discovered. The surgeon was able to repair it, and his young patient fully recovered.

Amy has not had a day of joint pain since.

CONCLUSION

Vast improvements have been made in the diagnosis and treatment of TMJ disorders. As more people come to know about the disorders and as information is shared within the medical community, TMJ sufferers should be able to expect timely and effective treatment for their pain. Then they can begin the process of returning to a healthful and meaningful life.

TMJ disorders are complex. They deserve and indeed demand serious attention. It is time to put an end to the suffering and anxiety that so many TMJ sufferers experience. I hope this book helps readers by answering questions, allaying fears, describing treatments, and offering hope for a brighter pain-free future.

GLOSSARY

Acupressure—An ancient Chinese method of pain relief that appears to effectively relieve muscle spasm when used by a trained physical therapist.

Analgesic—A pain reliever that can range from over-the-counter aspirin to prescription narcotics.

Ankylosis—Permanent freezing of the jaw joint. This can occur when a traumatic injury results in bleeding into the retrodiscal tissue.

Articular disc—Rounded, fibrous cartilage that forms a flexible cushion between the condyle and the temporal bone in the jaw. It is attached to the condyle by ligaments.

Arthrogram—A diagnostic test that gives a picture of the jaw joint. A liquid dye is injected into the joint, and X rays are taken.

Arthritis—Inflammation of the joints and muscles, causing stiffness and/or pain on movement.

Arthroscopy—A relatively new surgical technique that enables surgeons to look inside the TM joint with a tiny microscope. The technique was originally used on the knee joint but has been adapted for use on the jaw joint.

Auriculotemporal nerve—The nerve that runs through the TM joint. It helps to control function and monitor sensation.

Biofeedback—A method of controlling normally automatic body functions such as muscle tension and heart rate.

Bite plate—A dental appliance made for the mouth that prevents the jaws from closing fully. This allows the jaws to rest and prevents clenching. It has proven to be a very effective treatment for TMJ disorders.

Cap—See "Crown."

CAT scan—A highly sophisticated method of X ray that can be used to photograph the jaw joint. *CAT* is an acronym for "computerized axial tomography."

Crown—A type of restorative dentistry in which an artificial cap is placed over a tooth that has been worn, damaged, or ground down.

Chiropractor—A health practitioner who manipulates and adjusts the body (usually the spinal column).

Condyle—A knoblike bone at the end of the mandible. The condyle rotates and slides down and forward when the mouth is opened.

Cranium—The top part of the skull. It encloses the brain.

Doppler—An electronic device that uses sound waves to pick up and amplify sounds. The Doppler is sometimes used to listen to clicking and popping noises in the jaw joint.

Electromyography (EMG)—A test to determine the electrical output of the muscles. It can be used diagnostically to discover disease of the muscles and peripheral nerves.

Hypertension headache—A headache that strikes people who have high blood pressure. The pain is a generalized, hatband type of ache. It is most severe in the morning.

Magnetic Resonance Imaging (MRI)—A sophisticated diagnostic test that can give a good picture of the TM joint. It does not involve any radiation.

Malocclusion—A bad bite, due to mismatched jaws or crooked, missing, or misaligned teeth.

Mandible—The lower jaw.

Migraine—A debilitating vascular headache that strikes only one side of the head. It is sometimes preceded by an aura, including visual and speech disturbances.

Myofascial pain dysfunction (MPD)—a muscle disorder that can cause headache, neckache, toothache, and/or earache. It is caused by acute muscle fatigue.

Night guard—see "Bite plate."

Neuron—The fundamental part of nerve tissue.

Occlusal appliance—See "Bite plate."

Open joint surgery—Surgery that involves making a two-inch incision at the hairline, just in from the ear, to reach and work on the TM joint.

Orthodontics—A branch of dentistry that deals with and corrects irregularities of the teeth and malocclusion.

Orthognathic surgery—Surgery performed on the bones of the jaw.

Retrodiscal tissue—Connective tissue located just behind the disc in the TM joint. It contains many blood vessels and nerves.

Retrodiscitis—Inflammation of the soft tissues of the TM joint.

Sinus headache—A headache caused by a clogged sinus passage.

Splint—See "Bite plate."

Temporal arteritis—A headache caused by inflamed arteries in the head and neck. It demands immediate medical attention.

Tension headache—A generalized, dull ache caused by a tightness in the head, face and neck muscles.

Tic douloureux—A rare but serious nervous-system disease that most commonly affects women over the age of fifty-five.

Transverse friction massage—A special type of deep massage that is used by physical therapists to break up muscle spasm.

INDEX

acupressure, 57

adhesions (scar bands), 80

age range of TMJ sufferers, 6–7

aggravations, reducing stress from, 91

"all in the head," 11–12
case history, 94

American Association of Oral and Maxillofacial Surgeons, 83

American Board of Oral and Maxillofacial Surgery, 84

American Dental Association, 6, 30, 84

anesthesia
as diagnostic tool, 47
as trigger point injection, 66

ankylosis, 25

antianxiety drugs, 70

antidepressants, 70–71

antiinflammatory drugs, 69

anxiety
dealing with, 70
pain and, 88

apples, 68

AROM (active range of movement), 41

arteritis, temporal, 49

arthritis, 24, 49

arthrogram, 46

arthroscope, 80

arthroscopic surgery, 79–81
therapeutic value of, 80–81

arthrotomogram, 46

articular disc, 9
stress and, 22

articular fossa, 8
bad bite and, 20

aspirin, 69
dependency on (case history), 97–98

athletics, 91–92

Ativan, 70

auricular disc, see disc, auricular

auriculotemporal nerve, 10

automobile accident, TMJ injury from, 24

backache, 14

back strain, posture and, 23

bad bite, see malocclusion

bagels, 17, 55

bath, as stress reducer, 91

behavior modification, 57–58

biofeedback, 58

bite plate, 61, 62–65
in case histories, 94–95, 96, 97

bone
coronoid, 57
jaw, see TMJ
mandible, 8
temporal, 8

braces, dental, 74–75

breathing exercise, 90

bridge, dental, 73

caffeine, pain and, 67
caffeine-withdrawal headache, 49–50
calendar, as stress reducer, 90
candy, 67, 68
canulas, 80
cap, dental, 73
caramels, 68
case histories, 94–100
casseroles, 68
CAT scan, 44
causes of TMJ disorders, 19–27
cavities, TMJ and, 42
cheek, pain in, 14
chewing, 7
    pain with, 14, 17
chewing gum, 67
chewing system, 9–10
chewy foods, 67–68
chiropractor, 29
chronic pain patients, 88
clenching of teeth, 21–23, 90
clicking, 13, 14, 16, 18
    seriousness of, 51–52
    test for, 41
clinics, TMJ, 33
Clinoril, 69
Columbia-Presbyterian Medical Center (New York City), 38
condyles, 8
    malocclusion and, 20
    stress and, 20, 22
    trauma and, 24
conservative treatment
    as diagnostic tool, 47–48
    surgery and, 78
coronoid bone, 57
costs, 35–36, 84–85
cranium, 8

crown, dental, 73
custard, 68

definition of TMJ disorder, 6
dental society, for surgeon reference, 84
dental surgeon, 80
dental work, TMJ disorder and, 25–26, 92–93
dentist
    selection of, 30–31
    as TMJ specialist, 28–29, 30, 34
dentures, 73
depression, pain and, 88
diagnosis, 37–50
    conservative treatment as tool for, 47–48
    difficulty of, 7, 10–18, 48
    importance of, 50
    patient's role in, 38–39, 42
diet
    liquid, 67
    soft-food, 67–68, 81
disc, articular, 9
    displacement of, 16, 17, 77
    slippage, 7, 16, 41
    stress and, 22
    tearing or perforation of, 77
    trauma, 24
disc fluid, 16
disc plication, 81
dizziness, 14
doctor, role of, 28–36, 38–39
Dolobid, 69
Doppler, 41, 43
drug addiction, medication and, 68–69, 70
drug therapy, 68–71

ears, 17, 40, 41–42
eating
    head position for, 55
    pain with, 14, 17
egg-crate pillow, 55
Elavil, 70
electro-myographic (EMG) study, 47
equilibration, 72
exercise, 56, 90, 92
eyes, 17, 40, 49–50

facial pain, 10–12, 14, 17
fall, injury from, 24
false teeth, 73
family, effect of illness on, 88–89
fatigue, 10
feeling neurons, 9
fist fight, injury from, 24
Flexeril, 69
foods
    to avoid, 55, 67–68
    to try, 68
forehead, sensitivity in, 18
fruit, cooked, 68

gender distribution of TMJ disorder, 6–7, 26–27
general practitioner, 29
gold onlays, 72
grinding of teeth
    dental procedure, 72
    habit, 21–23, 42, 90, 98–99
grinding noise, 16
gum chewing, 55, 67

hard candies, 67
hard rolls, 67
hash, 68

head, positioning of, 54–56
headache, 14, 15, 17, 24, 48–50, 92
head trauma, 49–50
heart murmur, 27
heat, for pain relief, 59
help, learning to ask for, 89
hero sandwiches, 55
hunger headache, 49–50
hypertension headache, 48

ice and heat treatment, 59
ice cream, 68
imagery, mental, as stress reducer, 90
implants, dental, 74
inflammation, 7, 10
injections, trigger point, 66
injury, see trauma
insurance, 35–36, 85–86
isokinetic machine, 59

jaw
    acupressure point in, 57
    direct blow to, 24
    locking of, 17
jawbone
    displacement of, 24
    reshaping of, 82
    sensitivity in, 18
    structural defects in, 77
jaw joint, see TMJ
jaw movement, limitation of, 14, 18
jaw muscles
    soreness in, 16
    stress and, 22
joint, temporomandibular, see TMJ
journal, as stress reducer, 91

laser, in arthroscopic surgery, 80
learning to say no, 91
lifting, proper positioning for, 55
ligaments, 9
light, sensitivity to, 40
liquid diet, 67
local anesthesia, 47
locking of the jaw, 17
lupus, 24
lysing, 80

magnetic resonances imaging, see MRI
malocclusion (bad bite), 10
    equilibration for, 72
    orthodontics for, 61–65
    stress and, 19–20, 23
    TMJ disorders and, 61
mandible, 8
mashed potatoes, 68
massage, 60
meats
    chewy, 68
    chopped or minced, 68
medical history, 38–40
medication, drug addiction and, 68–71
menstrual headache, 49
menstrually related pain, 40
mental imagery, as stress reducer, 90
mental stress, help for, 89, 90–91
migraine, 40, 48–49
mitral valve prolapse, 27
Motrin, 69
mouth
    difficulty closing or opening, 17, 18

pulling to one side, 18
    tight closing of, as cause of trauma, 25–26
MRI (magnetic resonances imaging), 44–45
muscles
    injections in, 66
    jaw, soreness in, 16
    of mastication, 9
    relaxing of, 90
muscle necrosis, 66
muscle relaxants, 69
muscle spasm, 7
    massage for, 60
    referral of, 11
muscle tension
    caffeine and, 67
    posture and, 23
    stress and, 22
myofascial pain dysfunction (MPD), 20, 22, 24

Naprosyn, 69
nearsightedness, posture and, 23
neck muscles, pain in, 14, 17
neck strain, posture and, 23
necrosis, 66
nerves, 9–10
    auriculotemporal, 10
neurologist, 29
neurons, see nerves
night guard, see bite plate
nonreversible therapy, 71–72
nutrition, 66–67
nuts, 67

occlusal appliance, see bite plate
onlays, 72
open joint surgery, 81
    diet after, 67, 81

oral and maxillofacial surgeon, 80, 83, 84
orthodontics, 61–65
    surgery and, 76
orthognathic surgery, 82
orthopedist, 29
orthotic, *see* bite plate
osteoarthritis, 24, 77

pain
    caffeine and, 67
    coping with, 87–93
    depression and, 88
    around ear or face, 17
    difficulty in measuring, 77
    family and, 88–89
    injections for, 66
    menstrually related, 40
    referral, 7, 11, 24
    rest for, 11
    surgery for, 77
    as symptom of TMJ disorder, 10–11, 14, 15–17
    upon waking, 17
    See also soreness
painful pretenders, 7, 48–50
pain treatment center, 34
palpation, 40–41
Pamelor, 70
pasta, 68
patient participation, 38–39, 52
perfectionism, stress and, 21, 91
permanent improvements, 71–75
personality, TMJ disorders and, 21
physical therapy
    forms of, 54–61
    goals of, 53–54
    for muscle spasm, 60
    postoperative, 81
    for posture problems, 23
    who can benefit by, 53
pillow, choice of, 55
planning, as stress reducer, 90
popping, *see* clicking
porcelain onlays, 72
posture, TMJ disorder and, 23
potatoes, mashed, 68
pregnancy, X rays and, 43
premenstrual syndrome (PMS), 40
PROM (passive range of movement), 41
Prozac, 70
psychiatrist, 88, 89
psychotherapist, 88, 89
pudding, 68

range of motion, test for, 40–41
raw vegetables, 55, 67
rebuilding your life, 91–92
relaxation exercises, 90
resting the jaw, 55, 67
retrodiscal tissues, 9, 24–25
retrodiscitis, 7, 24
rheumatoid arthritis, 24
Robaxin, 69

scar bands (adhesions), 80
scarring, laser for, 80
secretarial work, TMJ and, 23
self-assessment quiz, 17–18
sensory nerves, 9–10
sex life, TMJ and, 92
shoes, as shock absorbers, 56
shoulders, aching or stiffness in, 14, 17
sinus congestion, 17
sinus headache, 49
skull base, sensitivity at, 18

sleeping, position for, 55
slipped disc, 7
  case history, 96
soft-food diet, 67–68, 92
Soma, 69
soreness, in jaw muscles, 16
soup, 68
splint
  dental (brace), 74–75
  jawbone, see bite plate
sports, 91–92
spouses, sharing problems with,
    88–89
standing, head position in, 54
statistics
  on incidence of TMJ disorder,
    6–7
  on surgery need, 76
  on treatment, 52
steaks, 55, 68
steroids, injection of, 66
stethoscope, 41, 43
stress, 21–23
stress reducers, 90–91
stretching exercises, 56
support groups, 34–35
surgeon, selection of, 83–85
surgery, 76–86
  case history, 99–100
  conditions for, 76–77
  open-joint, diet after, 67
  orthodontics and, 76
  preparation for, 78–79
  qualifications for, 77–78
  questions to ask about, 82–83
  statistics on need for, 76
  types of, 79–82
symptoms, 13–18
  ambiguity of, 15–17
  self-assessment quiz on, 17–18

talking
  head position for, 55
  pain with, 17
team, treatment, 33
teeth
  alignment of, 10
  braces for, 74–75
  clenching or grinding of, 21–23,
    42, 90, 98–99
  crowns and caps for, 72
  equilibration of, 72
  false, 72
  implants, 74
  onlays for, 72
  pain in, 17
temple, pain in, 14, 18
temporal arteritis, 49
temporal bone, 8
tempormandibular joint, see TMJ
tendons, 9
TENS (transcutaneous electrical
    nerve stimulation), 60
tension headache, 15
therapy
  nonreversible, 71–72
  physical, 23, 52–61
thermogram, 45–46
tic douloureux, 49
tissues, connecting (tendons), 9
TMJ (temporomandibular joint)
  defined, 7
  described, 8–10
  purposes, 7
  resting of, 55, 67
  trauma (injury) to, 24–26
TMJ clinics, 33
TMJ disorder
  causes, 19–27
  defined, 6
  description, 6–12

TMJ disorder (*cont.*)
  diagnosis, 37–50
  help for, 28–36
  increased awareness of, 37, 38
  as multidisciplinary problem,
    35–36
  other disorders mistaken for,
    48–50, 95–96
  surgery for, 76–86
  symptoms, 13–18
  treatment, 51–75
  treatment goals, 71
TMJ–Facial Pain Clinic (New York
    City), 38
TMJ specialist, 29–32
tomogram, 46
toothache, 14
tooth problems, TMJ and, 42
transcutaneous electrical nerve
    stimulation (TENS), 60
trauma, TMJ disorder and, 7,
    24–26
  case history, 97
treatment, 51–75
  goals, 71
  length and cost, 52
  statistics on, 52

treatment team, 33
trigger point injections, 66
Trilisate, 69
tumor headache, 49

ultrasound treatment, 61
unscrupulous practitioners, 31–32

Valium, 69, 70
vegetables, 55, 67, 68
vitamins, 66–67

waiting, reducing stress of, 90
waking, pain upon, 17
weekends, relaxing on, 91
weight-loss programs, 92
whiplash, 24, 25
women, TMJ disorder and, 6–7,
    26–27

Xanax, 70
X rays, 43
xylocaine, 66

yawn
  pain with, 14
  trauma and, 25

ABOUT THE AUTHOR

Antonia van der Meer is a free-lance writer specializing in health and life-style subjects. She is the author of five other books including *Relief from Chronic Headache* in the Dell Medical Library. Her articles on child care, pregnancy, and other topics appear regularly in national magazines. She is married and has three children.

R𝑥 for Good Health

from Bestselling Nutrition Expert
Lendon Smith, M.D.

Over 7 months on The New York Times Bestseller List!

☐ **FEED YOUR KIDS RIGHT**
12706-8 $4.95

"Fascinating...a complete nutritional program to ensure a child's good health without medicine."
—*American Baby* magazine

First time in mass market paperback!

☐ **FEED YOURSELF RIGHT**
20066-0 $4.95

"The doctor's prescription seems to be working just fine!
—*Prevention* magazine